TEA CHINGS

TEA CHINGS
The Tea and Herb Companion

APPRECIATING THE VARIETALS AND VIRTUES OF FINE TEA AND HERBS

RON RUBIN AND STUART AVERY GOLD

MINISTERS OF

The REPUBLIC of TEA®

Newmarket Press
New York

Illustration credits: All illustrations by Gina Amador, except:
pages x-xi by Image Studio; pages 18, 20, 37, 38, by William H.
Ukers, *All About Tea* (The Tea and Coffee Trade Journal, 1935).
Illustrations on pages 13, 20, 27, 35, 61, 62 are based on draw-
ings by William H. Ukers in *All About Tea*. Recipe credits: Page
43, from *Chai: The Spice Tea of India*, by Diana Rosen (© by
Diana Rosen; used with permission from Storey Publishing
LLC), and page 74 by Gina Amador.

1 2 3 4 5 6 7 8 9 10

Library of Congress Cataloging-in-Publication Data

Rubin, Ron, 1949-
    Tea-chings : appreciating the varietals and virtues of fine tea and
herbs / [Ron Rubin, Stuart Avery Gold]. — 2nd ed.
    p. cm.
    Includes index.
    ISBN 1-55704-491-0
    1. Tea. 2. Cookery (Tea) I. Gold, Stuart Avery. II. Title.
    TX817.T3 .R83 2002
    641.3'372—dc21
                                        2001008058

QUANTITY PURCHASES

Companies, professional groups, clubs, and other organizations
may qualify for special terms when ordering quantities of this
title. For information, write the Special Sales Department,
Newmarket Press, 18 East 48th Street, New York, NY
10017, call (212) 832-3575, fax (212) 832-3629, or e-mail
mailbox@newmarketpress.com.

www.newmarketpress.com

Manufactured in the United States of America

At the authors' request, this book has been printed
on acid-free paper.

To all, a cup of humanity.

Contents

A MESSAGE FROM THE MINISTER OF TEA

So many teas . . . so little time.

How does one come to know all the answers?

What is tea?

Where does it come from?

How is it produced?

Why is it good for your health?

What is the difference between green, black, and Oolong tea?

How do you brew the perfect cuppa?

What herbs make the most delicious herb teas?

In our travels outside The Republic of Tea, we have heard these questions many times. Like tea itself, questions diverse in flavor and effect. Realizing our future lies in a well-informed citizenry, we decided it was time to share the answers.

Originally intended for our Republic's Ambassadors, I have authorized that the Great Hall of Ministers officially declassify all information engendering the legend and the mystery of the brewable leaves—tea from the little *Camellia sinensis* bush, and herbs from a host of other useful and flavorful plants. In the spirit of public service, we extend this companion guide as an open invitation to journey the road to the rich experience that tea offers.

Tea, after all, is a drink of subtlety. Anyone can become an expert—all it takes is a little attention. These pages can help.

The REPUBLIC of TEA

Dear Fellow People of Tea,

Imagine a place of unparalleled tranquility. Where life still flows at a slower, more gentle pace. A place far removed from a world made jittery from change, volume, and too much of the dark oily opiate of roasted beans. It's a place you can travel to without really leaving. No jets to board, no miles to drive. A place where all matter of baggage blissfully disappears. A place that waits patiently for you to discover the aesthetic tranquility of illumination.

The path begins with the first step of savoring life in a gentler, wiser way—sip by sip rather than gulp by gulp. Every cup of fragrant steaming tea is a journey of beguiling enrichment and discovery. Entering true tea you find yourself transported among the divine and varied foliage of the *Camellia sinensis* bush, where tea, the ancient friend to mind and body, awakens you to an eternity of joy and contentment. Within the stillness, between the first sip and the last, the world becomes new again.

Throughout these pages an auspicious journey awaits. For sage or novice, this pilgrimage beckons all to celebrate what has been revered for thousands of years as the drink of humanity. Here we offer an enumeration celebrating the haunting boundlessness of the great gift of the leaf. Its rich and honored history, its botanical benefits, its complexities, spirit, and art.

Here within the youth of the water and the poetry of the leaf do we meet our truest essence. With each sip of tea, we engage the tangible and imaginary; welcoming the effulgent light of unmoored thought, erudition shines. This is drinking tea.

Yours in the Spirit of Change,

Travel

The Minister of Travel

Part One

TEA

Camellia sinensis

chapter 1.

THE PLANT
CALLED TEA

THERE ARE many teas, but only one plant.
That plant is *Camellia sinensis*. The Latin name
means "Chinese camellia," and this evergreen
shrub is indeed a relative of the flowering camellia bush
well known to gardeners. Incredible as it seems, the few
leaves that sprout at the very top of this plant, and this
plant only, are what is transformed into *all* types of
tea—black, green, and Oolong. (*Camellia sinensis* leaves
are not, however, the source of "herb teas," about which
more in Part Two.)

One plant...many teas. How can it be? This is the
fascinating mystery of tea. To understand it, consider a
comparison to wine. One species, *Vitis vinifera*, accounts for nearly all the world's production of wine,
from delicate Chardonnay to sparkling Champagne,
from sturdy *vin ordinaire* to complex Bordeaux—one

species, many varietals, and many production techniques. So it is with tea.

As with wine grapes, subtle differences of soil, elevation, and climate all affect the character of tea cycles.
The whims of weather cycles—early monsoon, late
monsoon, drought—are also crucial. And a great deal of
tea's character comes from the choice of leaves picked
and how they are treated, or "manufactured," after they
are plucked from their branches.

There are two main *Camellia sinensis* types: the small-
leafed China type or "jat" (*Camellia sinensis sinensis*) and
the large-leafed, and far more prevalent, Assam jat
(*Camellia sinensis assamica*, named for a tea-growing
region in India). These two types and their hybrids
comprise some 3,000 varietals—low-growing and
mountain-loving, delicate and robust. All of them contain caffeine in their leaves, to varying degrees, which
accounts for tea's rightful reputation as a mild stimulant.

In the wild, the *Camellia sinensis* bush can grow as
tall as 60 feet. Cultivated tea bushes are pruned to between three and five feet. From the air, the plantings
resemble a dense green mat, faintly furrowed by the
narrow, serpentine paths between the bushes. The
mountainous terrain in Darjeeling, in northern India,
and the hilly gardens of Ceylon (Sri Lanka) require in-
tricate paths of plantings that curve along mountain
slopes. Even if it spans hundreds of acres, a tea plantation is called a garden.

From each plant, only the first few inches of growth—
in the finest teas, just the first two leaves and a single

bud, where the flavor is concentrated—are destined for transformation into the sublime beverage we know as tea.

> THE WHOLE PROBLEM WITH CIVILIZATION IS THAT WE'VE BEEN TRYING
> TO SQUEEZE THE MIND INTO THE BRAIN AND IT WON'T FIT.
> THE GREAT GIFT OF THE LEAF IS THAT IT RELAXES THE BRAIN, FREEING IT
> TO FLOAT TO ITS TRUE HOME IN THE BOUNDLESS AND INEXHAUSTIBLE—
> THE SUBLIME STATE WE CALL TEAMIND.
> —THE MINISTER OF LEAVES

Where Is Tea Grown?

Camellia sinensis is indigenous to that part of the world we now call China, Tibet, and northern India. Over the centuries it has been transplanted far and wide, and today is successfully cultivated within a geographic belt that runs between the Tropics of Cancer and Capricorn—from the equator to 42° north.

Worldwide, about 6 million acres are planted with tea—a paltry amount, really. (Wine grapes cover 20 times that much land.) Those gardens have produced 6.5 billion pounds, or 2.95 billion kilograms, of tea in a single year.

Although tea cultivation came relatively late to India, during the nineteenth century, that country is the world's leading tea producer. Tea is grown from Russia to Argentina, from Kenya to Turkey. Experimental

Ancient wild tea tree

tea gardens once thrived in South Carolina, around the turn of the nineteenth century, but proved commercially impractical. Since the 1990s, there has been a small revival of interest in U.S. tea growing, with some of the most interesting experiments taking place in Oregon and Washington, considerably farther north than the classic "Tea Belt."

LEADING PRODUCERS OF TEA BY COUNTRY

India
China
Sri Lanka (Ceylon)
Kenya
Turkey
Indonesia
Japan
Vietnam
Argentina
Malawi
Tanzania
Taiwan (Formosa)
Zimbabwe

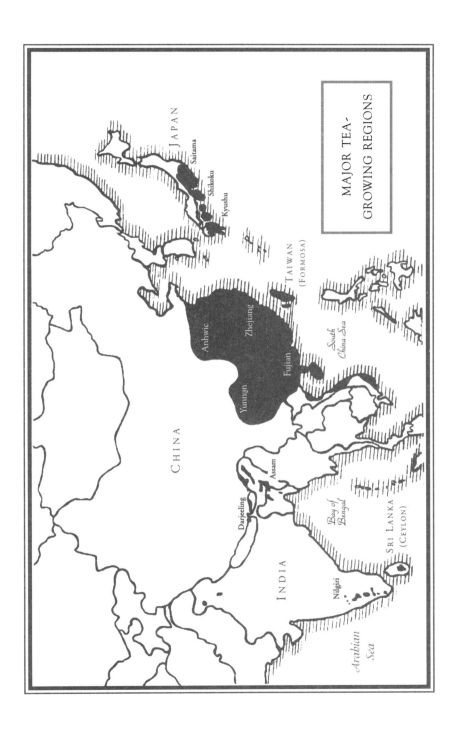

MAJOR TEA-GROWING REGIONS

JAPAN

Saitama

Shikoku

Kyushu

TAIWAN
(FORMOSA)

Anhwie

Zhejiang

Fujian

Yunnan

South
China Sea

CHINA

Assam

Darjeeling

Bay of
Bengal

SRI LANKA
(CEYLON)

INDIA

Nilgiri

Arabian
Sea

THE SOIL.
THE ELEVATION.
THE CLIMATE.
THE SUNSHINE.
THE RAIN.
THE TEA.

BODY.
MIND.
EQUANIMITY.
HARMONY.
WATER.
TEA.
—THE MINISTER OF GARDENS

Experiments aside, the great teas of the world come from just a few countries: China, Taiwan (Formosa), Sri Lanka (Ceylon), Japan, and India.

Climate, Soil, and Elevation

A hardy bush, the tea plant thrives in tropical and subtropical climates with warm temperatures, abundant shade (often provided by strategically planted shade trees), and generous rainfall—80 to 100 inches a year. Seasonal monsoons, which bring warm, torrential rains, cause the leaves to grow prolifically, but diminish their distinct flavor.

The finest teas, as a rule, grow at elevations between 3,000 to 6,000 feet; the cooler temperatures at these elevations retard the leaves' growth and allow them to develop their full qualities. Small variations in elevation can produce remarkable differences in the size and quality of the leaf: Within a single plantation, tea bushes grown at 4,000 feet and at 5,000 feet may produce leaves of utterly different character. Generally speaking, the higher a tea is grown, the thinner its body and the more concentrated its flavor.

Proximity to the equator also affects *Camellia sinensis*. Teas grown in the tropical regions of the world, such as Sri Lanka, are picked year round. Teas grown at higher latitudes, for example in Darjeeling, are picked only about six months of the year, during the dry periods following the monsoons.

How Does Tea Propagate?

Camellia sinensis reproduces by cross-pollination: The flowers of one plant transfer their pollen to those of another. In nature, this process yields random and inconsistent results. So commercial growers either germinate seeds in nurseries, usually for about nine months, or create clones from mature leaves with axillary buds. The seed method produces plants with taproot systems, making them more resistant to drought.

Tea Varietals

Different growing areas are known for their specific tea varietals, just as different grape-growing areas are known for their varietal wines such as Pinot Noir or Chardonnay. Each tea varietal is a distinct subspecies with its own appearance and character. Nearly 3,000 tea varietals have been identified and cultivated. There are more teas in China than there are wines in France!

Some tea varietals are destined to be processed as green teas; others become black or Oolong. In addition, experienced tea buyers recognize distinctions among leaf size, shape, color, and fragrance. Some varietals, called "self-drinking," are best enjoyed on their own, while others are best when blended with other varietals.

So Many Teas, So Little Time

Black Teas

Black tea is derived from tea leaves that have been withered, rolled, fermented, then fired:

Assam (India)
Ceylon (Sri Lanka)
Darjeeling (India)
Keemun (China)
Nilgiri (India)
Pu-erh (China)
Sikkim (India)
Yunnan (China)

Some Popular Blends

English Breakfast
Irish Breakfast
Russian Caravan

Some Scented/Flavored Teas

Jasmine (China; green, scented with jasmine
  flowers)
Earl Grey (international; black, scented with oil
  of bergamot)
Lapsong Souchong (China and Taiwan; black,
  scented with smoke)
Many varieties of flavored teas

Green Teas

Green tea is derived from tea leaves that have
  been steamed, rolled, then fired:
Genmaicha (Japan)
Gyokuro (Japan)
Spider Leg (Japan)
Mattcha (Japan; used in the Tea Ceremony)
Sencha (Japan)
Hojicha (Japan)
Genmaicha (Japan)
Longjing (China; Lung Ching, Dragon Well)
Baozhong (China)
Gunpowder (China)

Oolong Teas

Oolong tea is derived from tea leaves that have
been withered, rolled, semi-fermented, then
fired:
Tie Guan Yin (Mainland China; Ti Kuan Yin)
Formosa Oolong (Taiwan, many varieties)

The Flush

The sprouting of new leaves and buds on the tea bush is
called a flush. Tea plants may flush two, three, or more
times within a growing season. In Java and Sumatra,
where there is no cold season, tea plants flush all year
round and are plucked every seven to ten days. In
mountainous regions, where it's cooler and the monsoons are spaced farther apart, flushes occur periodi-
cally. Some high-grown teas may have only a single
flush each year.

The most famous flushes comes from Darjeeling,
where each flush has its own distinct character. Within
a single tea garden, First Flush, Second Flush, and Autumnal Flush pluckings will yield remarkably different
teas. The first flush, in early spring, is celebrated like
the release of nouveau Beaujolais wine in France.
(Read more about Darjeeling flushes in Chapter 5 of
this section.)

Two Leaves and a Bud

Before it can be plucked, a tea bush must be at least three years old and three feet tall. But most of the bush is just a photosynthesis factory for the inch or two at the very top that matters to tea pluckers—and to tea drinkers. Fine, full-leaf teas are made only from topmost shoots—at most a single bud and two leaves

fine
medium
coarse

Plucking diagram

For millennia, tea was harvested only by hand. Where quality is paramount and full-leaf tea is respected, it still is. The process is beautiful to watch. The harvesters, usually women wearing straw hats and colorful saris or cotton jackets (depending on the country), wind gracefully through the bushes, expertly plucking the first inch of the bush with their fingernails and dropping the leaves and buds into baskets carried on their backs. They are paid according to the weight and the quality of the leaves they pick. Their baskets are emptied into trucks, which carry the leaves to the "factory."

Tea harvester

13

Where efficiency is more important than tradition, harvesting machines do the job. While some machine-harvested teas are quite good, the machines tend to be less discriminating than human harvesters, and often snatch not only "two leaves and a bud" but also the entire branch.

Does Leaf Size Matter?

Before they are processed, tea leaves vary dramatically in size. The fanciest Formosan and Chinese Oolongs are made from very large leaves that curl during processing but open intact when infused with boiling water. At the other extreme, Keemun, the celebrated black tea of Anhui, China, is made from plants that have a naturally small, compact leaf. Darjeeling teas also have naturally small leaves. So the answer to "Does leaf size matter?" is yes—although the natural range of different varietals can vary widely.

> THERE IS THE SIZE OF THE LEAF:
> ITS UNIQUE SHAPE,
> ITS UNIQUE COLOR,
> ITS UNIQUE FRAGRANCE,
> A TASTE ALL ITS OWN,
> AND IT CHANGES...SIP BY SIP.
> —THE MINISTER OF TEA

14

Processing Tea

Fresh-plucked tea leaves cannot be brewed and drunk. They must first be "manufactured"—a term that here hews closely to its Latin root, "handmade." Tea manufacture is by and large a matter of skilled manual labor.

Fresh tea destined to become black or Oolong is first "withered"—spread atop troughs covered with wire mesh for eight to ten hours in a cool room to remove about half of the leaves' moisture through evaporation. The leaves are now soft and pliant. Green tea is generally not withered but is processed immediately.

Next, the leaves are rolled. For this step, there are two options: **orthodox** or **cut-tear-curl (CTC)** (sometimes called crush-tear-curl).

In the orthodox, traditional method, the withered leaves are placed in a cylindrical roller that mechanically squeezes them to release their flavor. (Some teas, such as Jasmine Pearl, are even rolled by hand.) The leaves are left mostly intact and are characteristically long and wiry.

Since the 1930s, the orthodox method has given way in much of the world to the CTC method, in which the leaves pass between two sharpened rollers. The result is small particles that produce a quick-brewing, strong tea—perfect for tea bags. Most of the world's tea is CTC; the exception is Darjeeling tea, always rolled in the orthodox method.

Black Tea

To create black tea, the leaves are plucked and then treated in a four-step process:

☞ **Withering** removes moisture from the freshly plucked leaves so they can be rolled. Leaves are spread uniformly on trays or racks in a cool room for 18 to 24

Darjeeling

hours. By the end of this stage, the leaves have lost one-third to one-half of their weight through evaporation and are soft and pliable.

☞ **Rolling** the leaf, the second step, readies it for transformation. Fine, first-grade teas are rolled by hand, each leaf painstakingly curled through its length and twisted slightly in the process. This breaks apart the cells in the leaf, releasing enzymes that will interact with air and cause oxidation, also known (erroneously) as fermentation. Twisted leaves release their flavor more slowly when they are curled. Many teas are now machine-rolled—it is 70 times faster than the hand method. But hand-rolling preserves the "tip," which is prized as a sign of quality.

☞ **Oxidation** changes the chemical structure of the tea leaf, allowing key flavor characteristics to emerge. ("Fermentation," often used interchangeably with "oxidation," is an erroneous

16

term, as no alcohol is produced.) The rolled leaves are spread on cement or tile floors and tables in a cool, humid room. They are carefully monitored for the next one to five hours for proper color and pungency. An experienced eye and nose are required to know how much oxidation is enough, and how much is too much. Generally, the longer the leaf oxidizes, the softer its taste and deeper its color. However, green tea—which is not oxidized at all—has a very soft and subtle flavor.

❦ **Firing** is the step that stops fermentation. The leaves are placed in hot pans similar to woks or fed into drying chambers that maintain a constant temperature of 120°F. When done properly, the leaves turn black and lose all but one percent of their original moisture. Improper firing can cause an off color, loss of flavor and aroma, blistering, mold, and spoilage.

Finally, the tea is sifted, graded, and packed, either in wooden chests lined with foil or in multi-layered fabric sacks.

More than 90 percent of tea consumed in the United States is black tea.

Green Tea

Gu Zhang Mao Jian (green)

Leaves intended for green tea are plucked in the same manner as black tea. They are then manufactured in three stages, which are completed within a single day.

❧ Steaming or pan-frying occurs immediately after the leaves are plucked. The leaves are placed in a metal pan over a hot flame to render them soft and pliable. The sudden exposure to heat destroys the enzymes that would otherwise lead to oxidation. Depending on the time of year and the type of green tea being manufactured, there may be a short withering period before steaming.

❧ Rolling the leaves on heated trays to reduce their moisture content is the next step. Rolling can be done by hand—with the fingers and palms, and sometimes with the entire forearm up to the elbow—or by machine (the CTC method).

❧ Firing in large mechanical dryers is the final stage of drying. Fired green tea retains only two percent of its original moisture.

Some green teas produced for export are rolled and fired several times to increase their shelf life. Although this increases their shelf life, it may impair their taste and character.

Chinese firing pan

18

Green tea is then sorted by leaf size and packed. The finest and most delicate grades are often put into metal tins or vacuum-packed to preserve their freshness.

Oolong Tea

This process, whose name means "black dragon" in Chinese, is a relative newcomer in tea manufacture, developed in Formosa (Taiwan) only in the mid-nineteenth

*Formosa
Oolong*

century. Most teas from Taiwan are still Oolongs, although Oolong is also produced on the Chinese mainland. Oolong tea combines elements of both oxidized and unoxidized processes and is sometimes called "semi-fermented," although fermentation, as has been said, is not an accurate description of the oxidation process. To continue the comparison with wine, Oolong is the rosé of teas, neither white nor red but a little of each. Oolong's caffeine content is midway between those of black and green teas. The leaves are picked just as they reach their peak and processed immediately.

 ❦ Withering and a brief **oxidation** are combined, for a total of four to five hours in direct sunlight. The leaves are spread three or four inches deep in large bamboo baskets and shaken frequently, bruising the leaf edges to make them oxidize faster than the centers. As soon as the leaves begin giving off a distinctive fragrance—

19

compared to apples, orchids, or peaches—this stage is halted.

Hand-rolling tea

❦ **Rolling** by hand (orthodox method) or machine (CTC method) follows the withering stage.

❦ **Firing** halts oxidation when it is about half complete. Baskets full of leaves are moved in and out of the flames of a charcoal fire.

Finally, the tea is sorted for size and color and packed for transport in foil-lined wooden chests or fabric sacks.

Traditional method of transportation

White Tea

White tea, or *bai-cha* in Chinese, is produced from buds and leaves that are simply steamed and dried without being rolled or fired. This type of tea has virtually no caffeine and a subtle grassy flavor.

The rarest of white teas is made from leaf buds that are plucked on the day before they open. The processed leaves resemble silver needles or silver rain, two other names for this type of tea.

Some tea shops also offer "white peony," which is made by tying white tea leaves together into rosettes that "blossom" when infused with hot water.

Pu-erh Tea

Pronounced "POO-air," this tea category takes its name from a town in the Chinese province of Yunnan, which once served as an important tea-trading center. The term refers not to color—there are black and green Pu-erh teas—but to special processing that allows the tea to have a very long shelf life. In fact, Pu-erh is the only type of tea that actually improves with age; some Pu-erhs are still drinkable at 50 years old! In our wine analogy, Pu-erh is akin to brandy.

Pu-erh tea begins with Dayeh, a special large-leafed strain of *Camellia sinensis* that's grown in temperate regions and picked year round. Leaves from very old trees are the most highly prized. After the tea is harvested, it is withered like black and green teas. Then, still slightly moist, it's heaped into piles, where a natural bacterium in the leaves creates a reaction (rather like what occurs in a compost heap). The piles are constantly turned and carefully monitored to prevent excessive heat or moisture.

To create green Pu-erh, the leaves are partially fired to halt enzyme activity but leave enough moisture to allow them to continue their slow oxidation over time.

Black or "cooked" Pu-erhs, like other black teas, are allowed to fully oxidize before they're fired, producing a dark, rich infusion.

Pu-erhs have strong, distinctive flavors and are said to yield many health benefits. See Chapter 4 for more about Pu-erh teas and health.

Blended Teas

Although the very finest teas are single varietals, many familiar and enjoyable teas are actually blends of two or more types of leaf, or of a single type from different flushes or estates.

Tea blending is a well-established practice. In the 1700s and 1800s, fashionable Europeans combined Assam tea from India and Keemun from China to produce a lively breakfast blend. Partly to suit this acquired taste, and partly because the quality and taste of leaves from a single tea garden vary from crop to crop and season to season, tea merchants began blending their products to "smooth out" their inherent variations and to compensate for seasonal shortages. This practice is directly comparable to the practice of vintners who blend grapes from several vineyards.

The United States Tea Act of 1897 was passed to protect consumers from inferior teas that had been "masked" or cut with non-tea ingredients. The Federal Tea Tasters Repeal Act of 1996 repealed the law and eliminated the Board of Tea Experts who had been responsible for inspecting every tea shipment that entered the United States. Currently, tea is subject to the Federal Food, Drug, and Cosmetic Act and the Tea Importation Act; it is therefore illegal to import tea that lacks purity, quality, and fitness, as determined by the Food and Drug Administration's Secretary of Health and Human Services.

But blending was also irresistible to unscrupulous merchants, who adulterated their blends with used tea leaves, leaves from other plants, and even sawdust. As a result, many countries passed laws to protect consumers against inferior tea.

For more about specific tea blends, such as "breakfast" or "caravan" teas, please consult our Tea Glossary in Chapter 5.

How Is Tea Graded?

After tea is processed, it's sifted by machine or by hand to determine its size: whole leaf, broken or small leaf, fannings (very small broken leaves), or "dust" (what's left after everything else has been sorted).

Tea is also graded according to its appearance. Each country has its own grading system, but in general the leaves with the most "tip"—the very top of the plant— receive the highest rating. Black teas are graded with a complicated acronym system based on the term "Orange Pekoe"—pekoe from the Chinese word for "white hair" (which covers the tender leaves when they're plucked) and Orange . . . well, no one is quite certain.

Whole leaves

Fannings

Dust

23

(Some speculate the term came from the Dutch House of Orange, which monopolized the tea trade in the seventeenth and eighteenth centuries.) The grading refers only to appearance and not to flavor.

Green teas are graded by a simpler system. The highest grade goes to teas consisting of a bud and one leaf, followed by those with a bud and two leaves, a bud and three leaves, and so on.

A tea's grade has nothing to do with its processing method, orthodox or CTC. For that information, you must trust a reliable tea merchant.

WHEREFORE PEKOE?

"Pekoe," which appears in many grading expressions, is one of the odder terms associated with tea. The word, which rhymes with "gecko" (not "Rico"), comes from the Chinese word for "white hair," describing the downy tips of young leaf buds. Yet it is used to describe only Indian and Ceylon teas, never Chinese. And it refers not to down or tips but rather to the presence of whole leaves. "Orange pekoe," another frequently used and misleading term, has nothing to do with orange color or flavor. Early Dutch traders used it to imply nobility—it refers to the royal Dutch House of Orange, and should always be capitalized. Both "pekoe" and "Orange pekoe" are often misused on tea labels to imply flavor rather than as an indication of actual quality.

Tea Grading: A Partial Glossary

Orange Pekoe (OP): A fancy grade of full-leaf tea with no tip; leaves are thin and rolled lengthwise.

Golden Flowery Orange Pekoe (GFOP): Like Orange Pekoe, but with conspicuous golden buds. A slightly lesser grade is Flowery Orange Pekoe (FOP).

Tippy Golden Flowery Orange Pekoe (TGFOP): As above, but with even more tips. The absolute top grade, usually assigned only to full-leaf Indian teas from Darjeeling and Assam. Occasionally the numeral "1" or "2" will follow the acronym, signifying even finer grades.

Broken Orange Pekoe (BOP): A step below the full leaf—broken or small leaves. Can also be characterized as "Tippy," "Golden," "Flowery," or any combination.

Fannings (F): Very small broken leaves, about the size of pinheads. May be produced by either orthodox or CTC processing methods. CTC fannings are chunkier in shape.

Dust (D): Literally the bottom of the chest or barrel. The smallest broken leaf left over from the manufacturing and sifting processes. Also known as "sweepings" (although, contrary to rumor, not swept off the floor).

Pekoe Fannings (PF) and Pekoe Dust (PD): Teas produced using the CTC method specifically for better-quality tea bags. They are grainy or even chunky in appearance. They infuse and color quickly and tend to be quite aromatic.

The Tea Auction

Tea has been traded through auctions since 1679, when London established the first tea auction. The historic London auction house closed its doors in 1998, but tea auctions remain a lively and regular occurrence in India, Kenya, Sri Lanka, and other tea-producing countries except China.

Graded and sorted tea is packed into bags or chests weighing between 40 and 100 pounds. The chests or bags are assigned to chops (lots)—a "chop" is a seal that identifies a family or a business, or by extension a batch of tea.

When the tea arrives at the auction center, each chop is published in a catalog, and samples are distributed to registered buyers. During the two weeks before the sale, buyers and brokers "cup" the teas—taste them and compare their appearance, aroma, and taste to those of similar teas and to general standards. On the day of the sale, buyers congregate at the auction center to bid against one another. Two or three lots are sold each minute, in lots averaging 1,000 to 1,500 kilograms.

Fine and rare teas sell in much more limited quantities of as little as 200 kilograms (three to five chests). They are often bought immediately—or even by advance bid, as with wine futures.

About 35 percent of the world's tea is sold through live auctions; the rest (mostly finer or rarer tea) is sold through private sales. Recently, there has been some discussion about conducting international tea auctions through the Internet, but so far the logistics of "e-tea commerce" have proved too daunting.

Chinese tea caddy

The Price of Tea

Fine, full-leaf teas are usually not sold at auction. Their growers set a price—between $8 and $60 a kilogram, or even more—which is not negotiable. Once in a while, a very rare or exceptional tea comes along and commands a price some would consider outrageous . . . but which seems entirely logical to the overjoyed buyer.

Teas sold at auction are generally of average quality, and fetch as little as $1 a kilogram.

For the consumer, this means that tea is a very affordable luxury when calculated by the cost per cup. A pound of leaf tea produces about 200 cups, so even a very rare tea that sells for $300 a pound costs a mere $1.50 per cup—less than many other rare beverages.

Storing Tea

Tea is a relatively fragile commodity. Within 18 to 24 months after harvest, the volatile essential oils in the leaves evaporate, resulting in a loss of fragrance. Green teas are best drunk within six months after harvest. Delicate, first-flush teas, such as Darjeelings, are even more ephemeral, losing their best notes within just a few months after picking. The small, broken leaves and "dust" used in tea bags are the shortest-lived of all. Rolled teas, black or green, such as the pelletlike gunpowder tea, last longest because less of the leaves' surface is exposed to air.

Storing tea is not just a storage issue. It has everything to do with the flavor and delight that the tea offers. Oxygen, moisture, and alien aromas are all enemies to the delicate subtleness of tea. Fine teas are especially fragile and can easily be ruined by such elements. It's important to store tea in airtight containers, preferably metal, and protect them from exposure to light, humidity, and high temperatures. The Republic of Tea's tightly lidded tins are ideal for kitchen storage.

Two exceptions to the short-shelf-life rule are Keemun and Pu-erh teas. Both gain character as they age; for this reason, Keemun is sometimes approvingly called "winy." However, they should still be stored away from heat, light, and moisture.

Tea Bags

The tea bag was invented in 1908 by a New York City tea importer named Thomas Sullivan, who was looking for a way to promote his business. He spooned tea leaves into small silk bags, sewed them up by hand, and sent them to his customers, who were delighted by the convenience: they could put the samples, bags and all, directly into teapots or cups. The bags were just large enough to allow the leaves to fully expand and infuse properly, and they made it easy to remove the tea from the pot.

Sullivan got the message, substituted gauze for silk, and revolutionized tea drinking in America.

Tea from tea bags has several advantages: It simplifies removal of tea from the teapot, it needs water of only 190° instead of the boiling point of 212°, and it brews quickly. Unfortunately, bagged tea has developed a reputation (in many cases earned) for being inferior in quality.

The Republic of Tea emphasizes the complex character and flavor that comes from brewing fresh, natural, whole leaves; however, we do make available our best-selling teas and herbs in environmentally conscious,

unbleached, round pillow-style tea bags, free of unnecessary and wasteful wrapping, tags, string, or staples. Though we encourage drinking full-leaf tea whenever possible, The Republic offers the finest teas you will find in a bag so you can still enjoy great tea at work, on treks, while traveling, or wherever you may not have the proper brewing tools on hand.

Tea sack

Organic Tea

A small but steadily growing segment of the tea market, organic tea represents a commitment to the natural environment and human health. Certified organic tea plantations use compost and green manure, avoid pesticides, control soil erosion through contour planting, and use natural predators to control pests and disease.

Organic cultivation results in healthy tea plants—and healthier tea workers, who are not exposed to harmful chemicals.

India currently leads the world in organic tea cultivation—Sri Lanka is in second place, and China is third.

Decaffeinated Tea

All kinds of tea can be decaffeinated, although not completely: Decaffeinated tea retains about 3 percent of its original caffeine content, of 0.4 percent of its total dry weight. Manufacturers can choose between ethyl acetate caffeine extraction (similar to the process used to decaffeinate coffee) or high-pressure extraction with carbon dioxide, an odorless, flavorless, harmless gas. Carbon-dioxide decaffeinated green tea has the added advantage of retaining 90 percent of its polyphenols, the healthful antioxidants abundant in green tea.

For more about caffeine in tea, please see Chapter 4.

chapter 2.

A SHORT HISTORY OF TEA

Tea Around the World

TEA IS A universal beverage, consumed in greater quantity worldwide than any other drink except water.

But "tea" means different things in different places. In Britain and Ireland, the world's leading tea consumers, tea is black and hearty, usually made with leaves from Ceylon and India and served with milk (poured into the cup before the tea) and sugar. In China, tea may be made from long, flat Oolong leaves and served in a covered cup. Ask for tea in Japan, and you'll get green tea—and green tea only. A cup of Indian "chai" may be made with spices and canned milk. And if you order tea in the United States, you'll have to modify your request: iced or hot?

Tea was once the closely guarded secret of one country, China, and that is where we begin our international tour.

> THE MOUNTAINS HOLD THE SKY.
> THE MELTING SNOW CAUSES SILVER
> RIVERS CLEAR AND DEEP. FILLING MY
> POT WITH WATER FOR TEA, SOON I
> WILL TRANSCEND FROM THE REALM
> OF FORM TO THE FORMLESS REALM.
> IN A MOMENT OF PERFECT FLUIDITY,
> ALL ENTANGLEMENTS WILL CEASE.
> THIS IS DRINKING TEA.
> —MINISTER OF TRAVEL

Tea, Cha, Chai

If you're visiting a country and don't know the word for tea, you can safely make a guess: It will either be "tea" or "cha."

"Tay" is the word for tea in the Amoy dialect spoken in China's Fujian province, across the strait from Taiwan. Dutch traders there in the seventeenth century learned this word and brought it to Europe; "tea" is still pronounced "tay" in Ireland, France, Spain, Sweden, and many other countries. "Cha" is the Cantonese word for tea, which followed the overland trade routes into Russia, Persia, and India, and sometimes turned into "chai."

The Idiomatic Tea Lover

Common Expressions Derived from Tea

A nice old cup of tea (British): *A dear person.*

Chali (Chinese): *Literally, "tea gift," given to a young woman when she is engaged to be married. By extension, the engagement itself. No longer consists of tea.*

Cuppa char (British): *A cup of tea (using the Cantonese pronunciation).*

Hock nit kein chainik (Yiddish): *Literally, "Don't bang a teakettle." Don't make a big fuss; don't bother me.*

Let the tea steep (German): *Let sleeping dogs lie. Used in the 1920s.*

Na chai (Russian): *A tip in a restaurant. Literally, "for the tea."*

Not for all the tea in China (American): *Not at any price.*

Not my cup of tea (American): *A person, activity, or thing one dislikes.*

Tea-leaf (British): *In Cockney rhyming slang, a thief.*

TeaMind: *A calm yet alert mind, full of good questions and smart ideas, waiting to be born. A natural state often obtained by sipping the right tea.*

Teetotal (British): *To abstain from intoxicating drink. Invented by English prohibitionist Robert Turner in an 1833 speech urging listeners to be "tea drinkers totally."*

Tempest in a teapot (American): *Much ado about nothing. "A storm in a teacup" was documented in 1872; at some point the cup was promoted to a pot.*

That's another cup of tea (British): *That's a horse of a different color; that's another story.*

The price of tea (American): *The subject at hand, as in "What's that got to do with the price of tea?"*

With no tea (Japanese): *Said of a person who is "insusceptible to the serio-comic interests of the personal drama" (Okakura, The Book of Tea). Conversely, an overemotional person is said "to have too much tea in him."*

33

Tea in China

According to legend, the Chinese emperor Shen Nong (sometimes spelled Shen Nung), known as the "Divine Healer," accidentally discovered tea in 2737 B.C. A *Camellia sinensis* leaf blew into his pot while he was boiling water in his garden; when he sipped the resulting infusion, he declared it to have medicinal powers. In his medical book the *Pen Ts'ao*, Shen Nong said tea "quenches thirst. It lessens the desire for sleep. It gladdens and cheers the heart."

In fact, archaeological evidence indicates that tea consumption was already ancient history by the time of Shen Nong. *Homo erectus pekinensis*, who lived in Southeast Asia where tea bushes grow wild, was boiling water and eating wild tea leaves more than 500,000 years ago. Tea leaves are still eaten as food in Myanmar (Burma), where they're steamed or pickled to make salads.

By the twelfth century B.C., tribal heads in China were sending tea as tribute to King Wen, founder of the Zhou Dynasty. Tea was regarded primarily as a medicine for many centuries afterward: It was drunk for digestive orders and nervous conditions, and was applied externally to alleviate rheumatism.

Gradually, the Chinese learned to cultivate wild tea bushes and to enjoy tea drinking for its own sake. From then on, as this timeline reveals, tea truly began making history.

The Evolution of Tea in China

5th century A.D.: Sung Dynasty. Tea cultivation is widespread through China, though primitive and un-codified. Tea is prepared by drying and pounding raw tea leaves, compressing them into cakes, and breaking off pieces for boiling in water.

520 A.D.: The Indian monk Bodhidarma (or Daruma) is said to have traveled from India to China, where he taught Zen meditation. He fell asleep once while meditating and became so angry that he cut off his eyelids. Where his eyelids fell to earth, a tea bush sprang up, guaranteeing pleasant wakefulness to anyone who sampled its leaves.

557-589: Chin Dynasty. Tea propagation becomes more organized. Buddhist monks introduce tea to Japan. Tea in brick form is used as currency and in trade.

620-907: T'ang Dynasty. Tea's first "golden age." In 780, the poet Lu Yu writes the classic *Book of Tea*, in which he describes growing, preparing, and enjoying tea. Tea is "donated" as a tax to the emperor, and spring tea-harvest festivals become popular. Tea is prepared by steaming raw leaves, pulverizing them, and shaping them into cakes, which are easy to transport.

960-1279: Song Dynasty. Tea rooms and tea houses are created as so-cial and spiritual gather-ing places; tea drinking is elevated to an art form.

Brick tea

Northerners increase their production of silk to trade for southern-grown tea. Special ceramics for tea preparation and drinking are developed. Tea is prepared by drying and powdering fresh green leaves, then whipping them with hot water in a bowl. Results are bright green, thick, frothy, and strong. (This style of tea is still served in the Japanese tea ceremony.)

1368-1644: Ming Dynasty. The now-familiar styles of black, green, and Oolong teas make their appearance, and tea is drunk all day long. Yixing clay pottery and blue-and-white porcelain are introduced for tea service. Tea becomes an important trading commodity throughout Asia and with Europe. Leaves are used instead of powder for the infusion, round teapots become the preferred vessel for preparation, and small cups replace bowls for drinking.

Another important development occurs toward the end of the Ming Dynasty: Portuguese traders arrive in China and set up a base of operations on Macao, an island downriver from Canton. They are followed by the Dutch, and soon tea is being offered in the cities of Europe.

> *"There is not alone a single quality of excellence in the leaf,*
> *for one surpasses the other."*
> —*Matteo Ricci, Italian Jesuit missionary in China*
> *from 1583 to 1610, writing home about tea*

Gongfu Tea

Yixing stoneware pots were developed specifically for a tea ritual known as *gongfu* (or kung-fu), which means "skill and practice" or "patient effort." Typically used for Oolong teas, tiny Yixing-style pots are filled about one-third full with Oolong tea leaves, which are steeped for only about 30 seconds for the first infusion, and slightly longer for each successive infusion—up to six or more. The brew is decanted into a special stoneware pouring vessel, about 5 inches tall, to ensure consistency of the liquor. Guests sip from tiny cups scarcely larger than thimbles, as though imbibing fine liqueur. Although there are many special implements for this ritual—from a narrow bamboo tea scoop to a metal or ceramic water drainer—the point is not the ceremony but the tea itself.

Tea in Japan

Tea was imported from China into Japan during the eighth century A.D. The beverage was useful during marathon Buddhist meditation sessions, but it quickly became popular as a secular pleasure as well.

By 794, the Emperor Kammu had a tea garden designed into the new Imperial Palace. And by the fourteenth century, the Japanese nobility was participating in "tea tournaments," a competitive tea-tasting ritual. Tour-

Bamboo whisk

37

naments were referred to by the number of teas sampled—"ten bowl," "50 bowl," or even "100 bowl."

Tea cultivation came to Japan in 1187, when the Zen priest Eisai returned from a trip to China with tea seeds or plants that he grew at his temple in northern Kyusho. Equally as significant was Eisai's book, *A Record of Drinking Tea for Good Health,* which suggested that tea promotes longevity and spiritual harmony. The book was influential among Japan's ruling samurai class.

Tea house

To the Japanese go the credit for elevating tea beyond its medical and sensual delights to a metaphysical spiritual pursuit. A lapsed Buddhist monk named Shuko, living in the fifteenth century, formulated the cult of tea into "*chado*"—the Way of Tea. It is said that he attained satori, or enlightenment, when he suddenly realized that a bowl of hot water expressed the law of the universe. His disciple, Sen no Rikyu, perfected the tea ceremony, or Chanoyu.

Ritual, discipline, and philosophy combine in Chanoyu. The tea ceremony preserves the elaborate customs of the Chinese Song Dynasty, where it originated, while adding a uniquely Japanese paradox: Chanoyu requires years of dedicated study, yet also celebrates simplicity and communion between host and guest.

The peaceful tea ceremony originated in wartime. During the sixteenth century, military leaders would leave their weapons outside the tea room and attempt to resolve their conflicts over a steaming bowl of cha. The rules and courtesy of the ceremony engendered a civil atmosphere.

Every aspect of the tea ceremony is significant, from the design of the tea room (three meters square, and decorated very simply with screens and a scroll or flowers), to the way guests enter (through a low door, which requires guests to bow and thus feel humble), to the utensils (special yet very plain), to the tea itself (bright-green powdered matcha, whisked with hot water into a froth), to the movements of the server and the drinker. The ceremony can last as long as four hours and varies with the weather and the change of seasons in order to maintain harmony with nature.

The Japanese tea ceremony was brought to the United States in the early 1900s by Kakuzo Okakura, a philosopher and author of *The Book of Tea*, a brief meditation on appreciating "the beautiful among the mundane of everyday life."

SENCHA TEA CEREMONY

There is a second Japanese tea ceremony, sometimes called "tea without ceremony." Based on the Chinese gongfu tea ritual, the sencha, or steeped-tea, ceremony was developed by poets and scholars in the late sixteenth century as a way to return to the simple Chinese roots of tea drinking. However, sencha has developed its own rituals and is taught in special schools. Where chanoyu uses powdered matcha tea, the sencha ceremony uses green tea leaves—also called sencha, or, sometimes, the more expensive gyokuru (jade dew). The tea is steeped in a pot and served in tiny porcelain cups while guests admire the paintings and other decorative objects in the room.

From the beginning, the enlightened have felt honored when bringing tea to people—or people to tea—for tea has been a drink to be shared with others. Around the world at high tea in Devonshire and at age-old ceremonies in Japan, tea is brewed and sipped together with friends and family in rituals of hospitality and nourishment for both body and soul.

"The average person talks of 'drinking' tea, but this is a mistake. Once you have felt a little of the pure liquid spread over your tongue, there is scarcely any need to swallow it. It is merely a question of letting the fragrance penetrate from your throat right down to your stomach . . . Some complain that if they drink tea they cannot sleep, but to them I would say that it is better to go without sleep than without tea."
—*Natsume Soseki, in his novel*
The Three-Cornered Room *(1906)*

Tea in India

Today, India is the world's largest producer and consumer of tea. But tea-drinking came late to the Indian subcontinent, in the seventeenth century. That was when India began importing tea from China and Tibet, where the secrets of cultivation were closely guarded. Tea was an expensive luxury in India, consumed only by rich people.

By then India was a British colony, and the British, resentful of the Chinese monopoly, were attempting unsuccessfully to cultivate some stolen Chinese tea plants. They had a lucky break in the 1820s, when indigenous tea bushes were found near the border with Burma. Seeds from those plants made their way to the Commissioner of Assam, who ordered the dense, mosquito-infested forests of that region cleared to make way for tea plantings.

The project was formidable, as workers succumbed to dysentery, yellow fever, and malaria. Yet the British persisted, and today some of the world's greatest teas come from Assam and neighboring Darjeeling and Nilgiri.

About Chai

While the British colonials and upper-class Indians sipped fine Assam and Darjeeling teas, ordinary Indians developed a fondness for a different sort of tea known generically as "chai." Chai varies from region to region, but it's traditionally brewed with either green or black tea and a blend of spices such as cardamom, cinnamon, cloves, and peppercorns, and served with milk and honey. Sometimes the tea/spice mixture is actually brewed in milk instead of in water.

According to one legend, the chef to an Indian king created the first chai from the spices of the realm. The king was so enamored of the beverage that he decreed that it could be served only in his court. Not until long after the king's death did the recipe filter out to the masses.

Today chai is very popular in Indian train stations and open markets. Vendors known as "chai wallahs" call through the crowds—"Chai-ee, chai-ee"—and offer low-fired unglazed clay cups called "kallurhs" that impart a rich, earthy flavor to the chai. After customers finish their drinks, they discard the cups, returning the earthenware to the earth.

Chai has developed an enthusiastic following among beverage drinkers throughout the world. Inventive serving ideas abound: steamed, frothed, or iced; or blended with yogurt or ice cream to create smoothies and milk shakes. For more about brewing and sipping chai, please see Chapter 3.

Tea in Ceylon

Until the 1880s, tea was a rarity in Ceylon (now called Sri Lanka). Instead, Ceylon was famous for its coffee. Then two dramatic events occurred: A parasite destroyed the island's coffee crop, and the British grocery magnate Thomas Lipton came to visit.

The failure of the coffee crop caused a real-estate depression; Lipton bought four plantations and converted them to tea growing. Four years after Lipton's initial visit, his tea plantations and factories employed 10,000 people. A marketing genius, Lipton promoted his middleman-free product as "Direct from the tea garden to the tea pot." His name is still synonymous with "tea" for many tea drinkers around the world.

Chai Pie

1½ cups apple cider

½ cup brewed Assam Breakfast or other Indian black tea

3 tablespoons arrowroot powder

2 tablespoons freshly squeezed lemon juice

2 teaspoons pure vanilla extract

½ teaspoon ground cinnamon

½ teaspoon ground ginger

½ teaspoon ground cardamom

3 pounds apples, peeled, cored, and sliced

⅓ cup packed dark brown sugar

Prepared or freshly made double-crust 8" pie shell

1. Boil the cider and tea over high heat until reduced to ½ cup. Allow to cool.

2. Preheat the oven to 450°F.

3. Combine the cooled tea-and-cider mix with all the remaining ingredients except the apples, sugar, and piecrust in a large bowl, and stir.

4. Put the sliced apples in a separate bowl and coat with the sugar; add more sugar if necessary to coat the apples thoroughly. Stir the sugar-and-apple mix into the liquid.

5. Pour into the prepared piecrust. Cover with the top crust. Cut slits into the pastry top with a sharp knife. Place the pie on a baking sheet and bake for 15 minutes.

6. Reduce the oven temperature to 350°F and continue to bake the pie until golden brown, about 45 minutes. Serve with a ginger sauce or whipped cream.

—From *Chai: The Spice Tea of India*

Today, more than half a million acres of Sri Lankan land are planted with tea, and the island's capital, Colombo, is home to the world's largest tea auction. Almost all of the tea made here is black, and much of it is of the very highest quality. Interestingly, the Ceylonese themselves drink very little tea; most of what they produce they export.

> EXPLORE THE VARIANT PATHS OF THE WORLD, GATHERING WISDOM FROM EVERY NATURAL THING, SEEN AND UNSEEN. WITH EACH SIP OF TEA I WASH AWAY THE DUST FROM MY SENSES, ESSENCE BECOMES COMPLETE AND CLEAR. IN MY CUP I DISCOVER THE FLAWLESS PEARL OF TEAMIND.
> —THE MINISTER OF TRAVEL

Tea in Taiwan

Tea was brought to Formosa (now called Taiwan) in 1850 by an enterprising man named Lin Fengchi, who had imported some Wuyi Oolong from across the strait in Fujian Province, China. By 1869 an Englishman was exporting the first Formosa Oolong to New York.

Many of China's ancient tea traditions have survived on Taiwan, where refugees from the mainland fled after the establishment of the Communist Party. The old Chinese teahouse culture flourishes here, and some Taiwanese tea experts are helping to redevelop the mainland's ancient tea gardens.

Taiwan is famous for its Formosa Oolongs, the flat-leafed, semi-oxidized tea made from plants grown below 1,000 feet in elevation. Although most of the tea grown on Taiwan is consumed domestically, at least one Taiwanese trend is gaining a following overseas: "bubble tea," made with tapioca pearls meant to be sipped through an extra-large straw.

Tea in the Himalayas

Tea came to Tibet and other Himalayan countries during the T'ang Dynasty (620-907 A.D.), when Princess Wen Cheng, the daughter of the first T'ang emperor, married the Tibetan king. Dwellers on "the roof of the world" rarely ate vegetables, and tea provided welcome nutrients in their diet. Most Tibetan tea came from China's Yunnan Province and became known as South Route Tea.

Because it is difficult to boil water at the high Himalayan altitudes, Tibetan-style tea is more like a greasy broth than the clear beverage consumed elsewhere. Tibetan yak herders added yak butter, barley meal, and salt to their tea, and trekkers in the Himalayas are still offered this hearty traditional brew, called *tsampa*.

Tea in Holland

The Dutch were the first Europeans to take a serious interest in tea. Around 1610, the first shipments of green Japanese tea arrived in the Netherlands, and soon thereafter, the Dutch East India Company established a tea-trading monopoly with both China and Japan. Other Europeans, and their American colonists, drank only Dutch-imported green tea for decades. The Dutch also introduced the ceramic vessels used to make and serve tea; it would take more than half a century for European artisans to unravel the secrets of Asian stoneware and porcelain.

Tea in Russia

In 1618, a Mongolian ambassador delivered a gift of tea from his prince to Czar Michael of Russia, who quickly became a devotee of the beverage. To satisfy his thirst, camel caravans brought tea from China to Russia over the arduous overland route. The difficulty of the passage made tea a luxury affordable only in large cities until the nineteenth century. By then, tea drinking was the height of French chic, Russians were enamored of everything French, and tea *à la française* became popular throughout Russia.

The camel caravans had a lasting influence on Russian tea-drinking habits. To lighten the camels' load, tea leaves were stuffed into bags rather than heavy wooden chests. During the journey, the cloth sacks took on the smoky scent of the evening campfires, and this smokiness became

Russian samovar

the identifying characteristic of "Russian Caravan" tea. Because fragile ceramic cups and pots could not be safely transported from China, the Russians devised the samovar: an all-in-one urn, usually silver or bronze, with a pot on top for brewing the tea, a large urn below for holding water, and a fire ring in the base. Traditionally, Russians make their tea extra strong and then dilute it with hot water from a samovar. It's served with lemon, and often sipped through sugar cubes clenched between the teeth.

> *"Ecstasy is a glass full of tea and a piece of sugar in the mouth."*
> —*Russian writer Alexander Pushkin (1799-1837)*

Tea in England

The Dutch had a stranglehold on British tea imports until the late 1600s, when the British East India company—a collective of wealthy British merchants with a royal charter to dominate trade—persuaded the Crown to ban the Dutch competition. Thus began the world's richest and most extensive tea monopoly.

Coffee vs. Tea

In the early seventeenth century, coffee—imported from the Americas via Spain—was well established as the hot beverage of choice. Some 2,000 coffeehouses had sprung up in London alone, selling coffee by the cup to an exclusively male clientele. The East India Company saw an opportunity to double its customer base by promoting tea as acceptable for women *and* men. In 1717, Thomas Twining (who founded the tea company that still bears his name) opened the first "tea-house" to men and women. Before long, tea was the preferred breakfast beverage in Britain, replacing the traditional favorite, ale.

Tea—Yea or Nay?

As with any vogue, tea attracted defenders and detractors. One of the most famous members of the former camp was Dr. Samuel Johnson (1709-84), author of the first English-language dictionary. He called himself "a hardened and shameless tea-drinker, who has for many years diluted his meals with only the infusion of this fascinating plant; whose kettle has scarcely time to cool; who with tea amuses the evening, with tea solaces the midnight, and with tea welcomes the morning."

Fulminating on the opposing side was John Wesley (1703-91), the Methodist reformer, who claimed that tea was a waste of money that could be more sensibly spent on food. Later, during an illness, Wesley tried tea—and became a convert.

Tea Gardens

In the mid-eighteenth century tea began to be enjoyed outdoors, in fair weather, in "tea gardens." Many such gardens were elaborate affairs with fanciful buildings, arbors, flowered paths, and lavish entertainments such as fireworks and concerts. The most famous gardens, at Ranelagh, Marylebone, and Vauxhall, attracted royalty, nobility, and social climbers, which added to tea's cachet. But tea gradually became a more domestic pleasure, and by the 1850s the last tea garden had closed.

Opium Wars

By 1800, Britons were drinking 5 billion cups of tea a year, and the Empire was facing financial ruin. Chinese tea merchants—no tea was yet grown in India—had no use for the heavy broadcloth that was Britain's primary trading good, so the British East India Company had to pay silver for tea. To stem the one-way flow of silver, the British turned to a product of their Indian colony: the opium poppy. The Company sold the Indian opium crop in Calcutta to other British firms that sold (or smuggled) it in China for silver. Actually, the silver never left Canton—it was simply banked for future tea purchases.

Opium poppy pod

The arrangement was convenient for the British but a fiasco for the Chinese, millions of whom became addicted to opium. In 1839, the Chinese emperor ordered 20,000 chests of opium burned on the beach at Canton. The British responded with a declaration of the "opium wars," which resulted in legalization of opium—a status it retained until 1908.

Afternoon Tea

The British custom of afternoon tea is credited to Anna, Duchess of Bedford, who in the mid-nineteenth century began serving tea, sandwiches, and pastries at 4 o'clock to fill the long hours between the big English breakfast and the customary 8 P.M. supper. Within a few years, the rules of afternoon tea became codified, governing utensils (china or silver, served on fine linens), accompaniments (small sandwiches of cucumber, egg, or watercress; scones and berry jam; toast with cinnamon), the tea itself (Empire-grown India or Ceylon), and attire (loose, flowing "tea gowns").

High Tea

The dainty portions served at afternoon tea were not of interest to Britain's working classes. Instead, they took to the custom of "meat tea" (or, illogically, "high tea")—a hearty meal consisting of substantial dishes served, of course, with tea. It often took the place of dinner, which was traditionally served too late for early-rising wage-earners of the Industrial Revolution.

Tea-time Today

Until World War I, the twice-daily tea break was still a fixture in the British home and workplace. Today, only afternoon tea lingers on as a cherished ritual; the visitor who drops in at four or five o'clock is almost always offered a "cuppa." Children are served "nursery tea," with plenty of milk and sugar or honey. A "cream tea," by the way, refers not to the lightness of the beverage but rather to the use of clotted Devonshire cream instead of butter on scones and toast.

Tea in Africa

Tea is an important cash crop in many East African countries, notably Kenya. The highest-quality Kenyan teas are full-bodied and can rival those of Assam; however, they are almost always made in the CTC rather than orthodox method. Cameroon, Malawi, Tanzania, Zimbabwe, Rwanda, and South Africa also produce tea—all of it black, some of it quite good, much of it destined for tea bags.

Tea is a popular beverage throughout North Africa. In Egypt, tea has been popular at least since the fifteenth century; black tea is preferred, served in glasses and drunk strong and heavily sweetened. In Morocco, a traditional hot beverage was made from mint leaves; British tea traders introduced green tea in the nineteenth century. Today Moroccan tea is a blend of the two leaves; it's served strong, minty, and sweet, poured in a thin stream from high above the table into small glasses.

Tea in the Americas

The Dutch brought tea to their North American colony, whose capital was New Amsterdam (now New

York), in the 1600s. Green tea—the only tea available—became a fashionable drink, sometimes flavored with peach leaves and sugar. By the mid-eighteenth century, the British were the dominant colonial power, the British East India Company monopolized the tea trade, and tea was the colonists' third-ranked import, after textiles and manufactured goods. As every schoolchild once knew, King George III raised the tea tax to pay for the costly French and Indian War, and independence-minded colonists cried foul. On December 16, 1773, a number of colonists dressed up as Mohawk Indians and tossed 340 chests of East India Company tea into Boston Harbor. The event, now known as the Boston Tea Party, was followed by similar rebellions, and eventually led to the Declaration of Independence—and to a longstanding American preference for coffee over tea.

In 1992, another rebellion took place in America, one that encouraged free and open immigration policies, greeting the worried, the stressed, and the obsessed with the divine and varied *Camellia sinensis* bush. A Tea Revolution offered to fill the cups of those fleeing fast-paced lives fueled by that somewhat darker brew. Requesting asylum, millions of coffee drinkers defected to

Clipper ship

the new state, seeking the road to savoring life in a gentler, wiser way: sip by sip rather than gulp by gulp. Soon everywhere, clouds of fragrant, full-leaf steam could be seen rising from the cups of the converted. Within the stillness, clarity, and calm, The Republic of Tea was born.

The United States did make two important contributions to the history of tea. The first, introduced in 1841, was the clipper ship, a radically redesigned sailing ship capable of sailing from New York to China and back in only 180 days—faster than the old frigate ships could complete a one-way voyage. This achievement allowed the fledgling U.S. merchant marine to successfully compete in the China tea trade. The British quickly built their own clipper ships, and soon great races between clippers were followed avidly by newspaper readers on several continents. But by the 1870s, the clippers were themselves superseded by a new and more economical development, the steamship.

The other American contribution to tea was actually invented by an Englishman, Richard Blechynden, who operated a pavilion at the 1904 World's Fair in St. Louis. His hot English tea failed to attract many buyers in the steaming Missouri summertime, so out of desperation or innovation he poured the tea over ice cubes. Today, iced tea accounts for 85 percent of all tea consumed in the United States.

Tea is grown in tiny amounts outside Charleston, South Carolina, as well as on experimental estates in

Hawaii, Washington, and Oregon. Several South American countries, including Peru, Ecuador, Brazil, and Argentina, grow tea, although so far it has not yet been of great distinction. Argentina is notable for one statistic: It is the source of 35 percent of U.S. tea imports. Most of that tea is of poor quality, and is used for inexpensive bagged tea.

chapter 3.

A NICE CUP
OF TEA

An Introduction to Tea Brewing

PREPARING TEA for drinking can be one of life's simplest and most satisfying pleasures. On the other hand, it can also be embellished with custom and ceremony. Whatever your preferred mode of imbibing, personal or social, meditative or celebrative, drinking

> CONTENTMENT OF THOUGHT.
>
> GOODNESS AND GRACE.
>
> HARMONY.
>
> WATER.
>
> TEA.
>
> TO THOSE WHO HAVE DISCOVERED THE PATH—
>
> SHARE THE CUP.
>
> —THE MINISTER OF TRAVEL

tea begins with brewing tea. And that takes effort and care, a chore easily enjoyed if you observe a few guidelines recommended by the Specialty Tea Registry (STR), an association of fine tea aficionados.

Water. Tea is, after all, mostly water, so the better your water quality, the better your tea will taste. Chinese tea expert Lu Yu stated that good tea was impossible without good water. He decreed that water only be drawn from the center of the Yangtze river. Luckily, we do not have to travel that far. Bottled spring water makes an excellent choice, or filter your tap water. Hard water can turn fine tea murky and chalky in taste. It can also bleach the leaves, compromising the experience. If you must use such water, keep the infusion time shorter. Start with water that is cool, to ensure that it's oxygenated. The STR has determined that the ideal water for tea has total dissolved solids (or mineral content) of between 50 and 120 parts per million and a calcium content of around 34 parts per million. Lower or higher levels will result in significant losses of tea flavor and aroma.

Measuring. The STR recommends 2 grams of tea for each 5.5- to 6-ounce serving—roughly a teaspoonful, although tea leaves' volume can vary. Sticklers will want to keep a kitchen scale handy until they feel confident enough to estimate.

Temperature. Water should be brought to a full boil—just. An extended boil will reduce the oxygen in the water, which in turn will adversely affect the tea's taste. Optimal water temperature varies for green and black tea; read on for more specifics.

Teapot. For brewing the tea, avoid metallic teapots, which can impart unpleasant flavors. Ceramic pots are most reliable. Some tea connoisseurs insist on different pots for black, green, and scented teas, but such distinctions are not really necessary. In any case, don't use scouring powders, or even soap or detergent, in your teapot—a good rinse with clean water will suffice.

Steeping. Green and black teas should steep for different amounts of time. Most green teas require a brief infusion, about three minutes; black and herb teas brew a bit longer. A rule of thumb: the smaller the leaf, the faster the infusion. Over-infused, or "stewed," leaves will often have a bitter taste. In general, discard the leaves after making your cup or pot (for exceptions, read

There are nine ways by which man
must tax himself when he has to do with tea:
He must manufacture it.
He must develop a sense of selectivity and discrimination about it.
He must provide the proper implements.
He must prepare the right kind of fire.
He must select a suitable water.
He must roast the tea to a turn.
He must grind it well.
He must brew it to its ultimate perfection.
He must finally drink it.
—*Lu Yu*, Classic of Tea

on). And for the best flavor, drink your tea within 15 to 20 minutes after infusing.

Experiment! Tasting tea is an art, not a science. Once you learn to appreciate true tea the world becomes new again. You find your beginner's mind and discover that there's a time for every tea and a tea for every time. Above all else, tea is a drink of subtlety. Anyone can become an expert, all it takes is a little attention. Each sip has the potential to deliver a serendipitous reward. Don't be rigid about tea. Try longer or shorter steeping times, different waters, different teas, and different tea tools and pots. Loosen up. Try new methods. Experience new moments. Explore. Enjoy. Practice makes perfect. So start practicing. Pick a tea. Brew a pot. Sip slowly. Repeat until you smile.

"Cupping" Tea

Professional tea tasters—brokers, agents, and buyers—are the most particular tea drinkers in the world. They evaluate two to three dozen samples at a single session, rating each on the consistency of its dry leaf; the aroma of the wet, infused leaf; and the color and taste of its "liquor," or liquid part of the brew. Experienced tasters can mentally compare as many as a hundred teas, and can quickly judge which teas will blend well with others. And they have an extensive vocabulary to describe what they're tasting (see box). Rather like wine tasters, tea tasters seek complex flavor characteristics—flowery, woody, malty, pungent—and especially prize mellowness (lack of harshness).

Tea-Tasting Terms

Some terms used by professional tea tasters to describe infused tea.

Body: The weight and quality of the tea on the tongue. Can be described as wispy, light, medium, or full.

Brassy: Strong and bitter; caused by underwithering of black tea.

Bright: Lively, fresh, and high quality.

Brisk: Opposite of "flat"; pungent without being undesirably high in tannin content.

Burnt: An off flavor caused by overfiring.

Chocolaty: A desirable flavor quality of fine Darjeelings.

Coarse: Bitter or overly acid; attributable to improper processing.

Dull: Muddy looking; the opposite of "bright" or "brisk."

Earthy: May be inherent to the leaf, or caused by damp storage.

Flat: Off, stale taste; usually a property of old teas.

Full-bodied: An ideal combination of strength and color.

Green: When said of black tea, refers to immaturity of character due to underoxidation or underwithering.

Harsh: Very rough in flavor; associated with underwithered teas.

Heavy: Low in briskness and very full-bodied.

Light: Lacking strength and depth of color.

Malty: Subtle, underlying flavor; a desirable quality in Assam teas.

Mellow: Smooth, easy, pleasant.

Metallic: A sharp, coppery flavor.

Point: Used to describe a leaf with desirable brightness and acidity.

Pungent: Pleasantly astringent; a good combination of briskness, strength, and brightness.

Self-drinking: A tea that can be drunk alone, without blending with other leaves.

Smooth: Rounded in flavor, pleasant on the palate.

Soft: The opposite of "brisk"; caused by inefficient oxidation or firing.

Vegetative: Grassy flavor, a desirable characteristic of some green teas.

It's not difficult to conduct a modest tea tasting in your own home. Try all green teas, or all Indian black teas, to learn to recognize subtle distinctions. Here's how to do it:

1. Arrange a half-dozen plain white cups on a kitchen counter after rinsing them vigorously with hot water to remove soap residue. Arrange each tea sample (in a plain container if you want the test to be "blind") behind a cup, and measure out a level teaspoonful of leaf into the cup. Observe the color, shape, and size of the leaves; a great deal of white or golden "tip" is often considered desirable, but doesn't necessarily affect taste.

Professional tasting cup (tea infuses for 4-5 minutes)

Tasting cup is then tipped into bowl

Quality of leaves and liquor is noted before tasting

2. Fill a kettle with cold water and bring it to the boil; when the water boils, fill each cup to the brim. Observe the leaves unfolding (in tasting terminology, this is poetically called "the agony of the leaves"), but wait until the cups have cooled slightly to spoon the leaves from the bottom to look and sniff. Write down your impressions as you go. Also note the color of the liquor—pale, chestnut, and amber are some of the terms commonly used.

3. When the tea is cool enough to drink, slurp it exaggeratedly from the spoon, allowing the liquor to spray all around the palate and the back of the mouth. Don't

THE LEAVES TAKE THE WATER, THE FIRST SIP
EMANATING WISDOM'S LIGHT. WHERE TEAMIND IS
POLISHED, IT SHINES, PERVADING THE UNIVERSE,
TEACHING US ONCE AGAIN—A TRUE CUP OF TEA
IS MORE THAN IT SEEMS. AND SO ARE WE.
—THE MINISTER OF TRAVEL

swallow—as with wine tasting, you'll be spitting out what you taste. (Experts use a special spittoon called a "gaboon.") Record the aromas and flavors you experience from each tea before moving on to the next.

Brewing Full-leaf Black Tea

Black teas are best infused with water that has been brought to a full boil. Use a little of the water to warm the pot and the cup, then discard. Pour the just-boiled water directly over the tea leaves, or over an infuser of your choice (see page 71). Allow the leaves to steep for about five minutes, more or less. (Here's where experimenting is valuable; some well-twisted teas require six minutes.) According to the STR, the water at the end of five minutes should be within a few degrees of 200°F. Black tea is best infused only once. Remove the infused leaves from the liquor to avoid "stewing" and creating bitter flavors. A tea cozy made of quilted or knitted fabric can be placed over the pot to keep the contents warm, if you like.

Milk and Sugar

Milk or cream in tea is a western European invention, introduced by the Dutch in the early 1600s and popularized in France a century later. The custom took hold in Great Britain in the 1800s, where milk was used to soften the

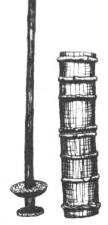

Tsampa churner

"edge," or astringency, of robust black teas from China and India. (Neither milk nor sugar is used in China, or with green tea anywhere.)

If you like milk or cream with your tea, it's best to follow the British custom of "M.I.F."—Milk In First. A few drops of warm milk are poured into the cup, followed by the tea. Historically, there was a practical reason for this custom: It kept the scalding tea from cracking fragile porcelain cups. It also prevents the milk from curdling.

The British also adopted the custom of sweetening their tea with a generous amount of sugar. After Queen Victoria visited Russia, her daughter's adopted country, Britons began offering an alternative to milk: slices of lemon, in the Russian manner.

Brewing Full-leaf Green Tea

Because of its delicate flavors, green tea requires cooler water than black tea. After boiling, pour a little of the water into the pot and cup to warm them. Then let the kettle sit for about ten seconds before pouring water on the leaves. In Japan, it's customary with very fine green teas to allow boiled water to cool to 160°-180°F. A larger proportion of leaves to water is used, and steeping time is reduced to only a minute or two.

Brewing Full-leaf Oolong Tea

Because Oolongs have such large, flat leaves, they can steep for seven to ten minutes without turning bitter. Finer Oolongs can be infused at least a couple of times using the same leaves. In the Chinese gongfu tea ceremony, Oolong leaves are "rinsed" with hot water; this rinsewater is discarded, and then the leaves are steeped in earnest. The Chinese say each successive infusion produces a different pleasurable effect.

THE MINISTER OF TEAS' METHOD

BOIL WATER.

INFUSE LEAVES.

DRINK TEA.

The first bowl sleekly moistened throat and lips,
The second banished all my loneliness,
The third expelled the dullness from my mind,
Sharpening inspiration gained
from all the books I've read.
The fourth brought forth light perspiration,
Dispersing a lifetime's troubles through my pores.
The fifth bowl cleansed ev'ry atom of my being.
The sixth has made me kin to the Immortals.
This seventh is the utmost I can drink—
A light breeze issues from my armpits.

—From The Song of Tea, *Lu T'ung,*
Chinese poet, eighth century A.D.

Making Chai

The spicy Indian beverage known as chai can be brewed in dozens of ways—if "brewed" is the correct term. Many chai recipes actually involve simmering black tea along with a mixture of spices that usually includes cardamom, ginger, cinnamon, cloves, and pepper. Sometimes fennel, vanilla, allspice, lemongrass, and coriander may be added as well. Condensed milk, sweetened or plain, is simmered along with the mixture. Recently, green tea and herbal chais have been developed. As always, the better the grade of tea, the more flavorful the final product.

Brewing Tea from Tea Bags

Make sure you use tea bags that have not been bleached or otherwise treated, because the chemicals used in those processes can affect the taste of the tea. Allow the bag to steep in boiled water almost as long as you would steep full-leaf tea; the shorter leaves in tea bags may infuse a bit more quickly.

Making Iced Tea

Iced tea can be made quickly or slowly. The quick method tends to produce a cloudy beverage; the slow method yields a crystal-clear liquid.

To make iced tea quickly, prepare a double-strength infusion of your favorite hot tea. Black teas are traditionally used because their stronger flavors hold up well when chilled, but green teas can produce interesting iced versions. Strain the tea through cheesecloth, if necessary, and pour into a pitcher or glasses filled with ice cubes.

The slow method uses cold water to prepare the infusion. Make regular-strength tea in a large jar with a tightly closing lid. Stir well and refrigerate overnight or leave at room temperature for six to nine hours. Occasionally invert the jar and then stand it right-side up again. Serve without ice.

A GREAT THING DONE IS NEVER PERFECT.
BUT THAT DOESN'T MEAN IT FAILS.
EVEN IN A PERFECT CUP THERE EXISTS A HOLLOW.
IT IS THIS EMPTINESS WITHIN IT THAT MAKES IT PERFECT.
WITHOUT IT HOW WOULD THE LEAVES TAKE THE WATER—
HOW WOULD WE DRINK THE TEA?
—THE MINISTER OF TRAVEL

Making Sun Tea

A very pleasant tea can be made using only solar energy. Place tea leaves—two teaspoons per glass—in a large Mason jar and add cold water. Seal the jar tightly and set in a sunny spot on a kitchen counter or outdoors. Every couple of hours, invert the jar and then turn it right-side up again. Depending on the strength of the sun, and the desired strength of the tea, your infusion should be drinkable—and warm!—in about six hours. Refrigerate any leftover beverage and serve cold.

Other Tea Drinks

Bubble tea: A novelty tea drink invented in Taiwan has gained a following throughout Asia, and in many North American cities as well. "Bubble tea," sometimes called "black pearl tea," is a festive infusion of hot tea poured over tapioca pearls. Often milk is added to heighten the contrast of white beverage and black spheres on the bottom of the glass. An extra-wide straw is used to slurp up the tapioca pearls, which are soft, squishy, and tasteless.

To make bubble tea, first boil tapioca pearls in water for 45 minutes, then cover the pot and steam them for 10 minutes with the burner off. Run them under cold water and drain. You can add some flavor by soaking them in honey and sugar. Pour hot brewed tea—black and jasmine teas are most popular, although chai and yerba maté are sometimes used—into a tall glass or cocktail shaker, add condensed or powdered milk, and pour in enough tapioca pearls to cover the bottom inch or so of the glass. Shake gently and serve.

Thai tea: A brightly hued orange-colored brew often served over ice in Thai restaurants is called Thai tea. The red leaves used to prepare this drink are grown in Thailand and, when infused, offer up a beautiful full-bodied orange color. Sometimes sweetened with condensed milk.

Bottled Tea: While sweetened, ready-to-drink bottled iced teas have been a mainstay on grocery shelves for years now, premium, upscale, bottled iced teas have entered the market as a healthier alternative. The Republic of Tea takes pride in creating a category that offers our refreshing realm of all natural, unsweetened leafy flavors for people who want purity and balance in their beverages. These varietal bottled teas elevate tea to its rightful place beside fine wine, pleasing the palate and complementing fine food brilliantly.

Other drinks: Tea can also be used to make smoothies and shakes. Spicy Indian chais make especially tasty blended drinks when combined with fruit, fruit juice, and yogurt or silken tofu. Or try adding brewed and cooled black chai to ice cream in a blender jar to make a delicious "chai shake."

Cooking with Tea

Long before tea was infused, it was eaten. Today, many sophisticated cooks use tea leaves to add flavor and texture to their dishes. Lapsang Souchong leaves lend their characteristic smokiness to Chinese tea-steamed duck or sautéed prawns; powdered green tea (*matcha*) is mixed with salt to create a crisp batter for fish; and Burmese tea-leaf salad uses marinated green tea as the base for a refreshing meal-ender or appetizer.

Teaware

While we value the wondrous taste of the leaf most, with a little attention, serving can become as rewarding as sipping. By practicing preparation and using the proper tea tools, the tea experience can be enhanced. The right teapot or cup can be both functional and pleasing and are easily obtained.

To serve tea, all that's required is a pot with a weighted bottom to keep it steady, a spout large enough for pouring, a means of straining out the leaves, and a cup. From these simple essentials a universe of teaware has evolved, from the cute and kitschy to the elegant and refined. The quality of the tools used in preparing tea enhances the experience and the tea. So let's get to know fine tea by imbibing fine tea with tools that delight and pleasure.

Yixing teapots: Pottery has been made near Yixing, China, in Jiangsu Province, since 2500 B.C. The distinctive Yixing earthenware—humble yet beautiful, made of a special purple sand clay that's porous yet able to withstand cracking—dates back to the Ming Dynasty (1368-1644 A.D.), when the Chinese were switching from compressed brick tea to loose leaves. A monk from the Jin Sha Temple made the first Yixing

Yixing teaware

69

teapot, a small vessel designed specifically for brewing loose-leaf tea. In basic design and function, the teapot has remained essentially unchanged.

Authentic Yixing teapots are made from refined Yixing clay that has often been aged for several years. The clay is sold to local artisans who may add minerals for color, or blend in different clay types. The clay is cut into plates that are slip-joined, shaped with special wood or bone tools on a potter's wheel, and fired at specific temperatures to allow the clay to develop its tea-brewing properties. As the pot is used, it becomes "seasoned" with the tea's flavor, allowing each successive brew to be a little better than the last. It's said that if you use a Yixing teapot for many years, you can brew tea simply by pouring plain boiling water into it! Look for the "chop," or monogram, of the potter on the underside of the lid or the bottom of the pot.

Gaiwan: This Mandarin word—the Cantonese equivalent is *zhong*—refers to a small, handleless tea bowl made of porcelain, with a matching saucer and lid. Invented during the Ming Dynasty and still used today, it functions as both personal teapot and tea cup.

To make tea in a gaiwan, place an individual serving of tea leaves in the cup, then fill four-fifths full with boiling water. Place the lid over the cup and allow the brew to steep for the recommended time. When infused in the cup, the brew can be sipped directly from the gaiwan, using the lid to strain out the leaves and keep the tea warm.

To sip, hold the saucer (it keeps fingers cool) and push the lid back slightly to uncover an opening. Doing this operation correctly, with one hand, requires some practice, just like using chopsticks, but is well worth the effort. When you're finished drinking, you can "read" the tea leaves in your cup!

Japanese ironware: The Japanese have used heavy cast-iron teapots, called *Tetsubin*, for centuries to heat water over open fires and brew tea for ceremonies. Pots are typically wider than they are tall, and may be embossed with designs inspired by nature. Modern ironware is glazed with enamel on the inside for easy cleaning.

Infusers: A wide variety of baskets, strainers, tea balls, paper filters, perforated tea spoons, and plunger pots make it easy to steep tea leaves for just the right length of time and then remove them. Never fill an infuser completely: It should allow plenty of room for water to circulate around the leaves and for the leaves to swell. Some teapots come with their own convenient infuser inserts. Basket filters—metal, ceramic, or plastic—allow the leaves to circulate almost as freely as if they were loose. Stainless-steel, gold mesh, and plastic mesh infusers are sized to fit into a teacup or pot and are easy to remove and clean. Tea balls are usually made of aluminum with small holes for water circulation, but often there is insufficient space for the leaves to luxuriously expand. Paper filters are like the filters used for that other brew, and are made to fit into a plastic holder. The plunger pot or tea press compresses the leaves to the bottom of the pot and holds them there allowing the free circulation of the leaves.

Samovar: This Russian invention is a large vessel,

usually copper, in which water is heated to boiling by means of charcoal in a pipe that extends through the center. A small teapot sits atop the urn, so that brewed tea can be kept hot. Tea (often with lemon added) is then served in glasses with metal holders.

Tea caddies: A tea caddy is a box or canister in which loose tea is stored. The word comes from the Malay *kati*, meaning "one pound," which is about how much tea a caddy could hold. Tea caddies became very popular in Britain in the first half of the eighteenth century, when they were an important part of a silver tea service. Wooden caddies were also favored; often they were inlaid with scenes of Chinese life. Many styles were fitted with a lock and key to prevent servants from filching any of the precious contents.

Teapoy: Caddies, mixing bowls, and other tea paraphernalia were stored in a teapoy, a small three-legged pedestal. "Teapoy" has nothing to do with tea; the term comes from an Indian word meaning "three feet."

WHO DRAWS THE WATER AND BOILS IT?
WHO SPOONS THE LEAVES FROM THE TIN AND
PLACES THEM IN THE POT?
WHO LIFTS THE KETTLE AND POURS?
WHO COULD BE A GREATER FRIEND?
—THE MINISTER OF TEA

Tearooms

Europe has long enjoyed the tradition of the tearoom, a civilized refuge from the bustle of urban life. Michael Smith, in *The Afternoon Tea Book*, fondly cites Sacher's in Vienna (home of the famous Sacher torte), Rumpelmayer's in Paris, Cova in Milan, Caf and Luitpol in Munich, and the Angleterre in Copenhagen. In England, there are elegant tearooms at Fortnum and Mason, the Ritz, and other fashionable venues.

Many U.S. cities have discovered the joys of the tearoom as well. The first "afternoon teas" were held in posh hotels and melded British and European customs into rich and elaborate banquets. Some hotels even offered tea dances, which first became fashionable in England around World War II.

As North Americans became more aware of Far Eastern tea traditions, a number of Asian-style tearooms began appearing in the U.S. and Canada. The new tearooms attract inquisitive customers who want to sample fine and rare teas while enjoying a calm, meditative atmosphere. Food may be served, but in our Republic, it plays a supporting role to the greatness of tea.

Like all republics, we must respectfully acknowledge that the power of our state resides in its tea-drinking citizenry. Unfair distribution of *Camellia sinensis* leaves stirred up trouble on the way to the formation of another familiar republic. In fact, tea has gone down in history as the first politically incorrect beverage. During the American Revolution's infancy, heavily taxed British tea was tossed overboard to steep in the cold waters of Eastern harbors, and drinking tea was considered a traitorous, counter-revolutionary act. Thankfully, times have changed.

Chamomile Cookies

These small cakes are especially good with a hot cup of chamomile tea. Makes two dozen.

> *1 stick butter or margarine, softened*
> *1 cup sifted all-purpose flour*
> *2/3 cup brown sugar*
> *2 medium egg yolks*
> *Grated rind of 2 lemons*
> *1 1/2 crushed dried chamomile flowers*

Cut the butter into the flour until the mixture resembles crumbs. Add the rest of the ingredients and, using floured hands, knead the mixture. Cover and chill for 30 minutes. Heat oven to 325°F. Roll the dough into 1-inch balls. Place on a pan and flatten with the bottom of a fork. Bake for 12-15 minutes.

How to Read Tea Leaves

Tea-leaf reading is enjoyed in many cultures. Its origins are mysterious, its rules nebulous, and its pleasures irresistible. Here is how the great Madame Oolong reads leaves in our Republic:

74

1. Brew a pot of tea, but do not use a strainer or infuser basket. A large-leafed variety such as Oolong is most "readable."

2. Pour the hot tea into a classic, rounded tea cup with a smooth white interior.

3. Drink the tea, sip by sip. While you do so, reflect on some question you wish the leaves to answer.

4. When you have finished, swirl the tea cup. Some say to use your non-writing hand; some say to swirl three times in the direction away from yourself.

5. Turn the cup upside down into its saucer.

6. Allow the leaves to tell their story. Pick up the cup, turn it right-side up, and gaze at the leaves that remain inside.

- ❧ Leaves nearest the rim relate to the near future.
- ❧ Leaves farther down describe the more distant future.
- ❧ Leaves at the bottom represent the very distant future.

- Many leaves in the cup indicate a full, rich life.
- One leaf stuck on the side foretells the arrival of a stranger.

The handle of the cup represents you (or the subject of the reading). Its relationship to the position of the leaves indicates one's relationships to the events or persons described by the leaves.

First impressions are important: They suggest an answer to the question you were thinking about while you drank the tea.

TOSS USED LEAVES INTO THE GARDEN.
THEY MAKE A FINE FERTILIZER.
—THE MINISTER OF SOIL

chapter 4.

TEA AND HEALTH

T EA DRINKERS HAVE many reasons to take delight in their beverage of choice. Not only is it available in many styles and flavor profiles, each affording a distinctly pleasurable experience, but for centuries tea has been associated with good health as well. Recent research supports this connection. Green tea in particular has been found to have protective effects against cancer, heart disease, and tooth decay.

> GOOD HEALTH IS TO THE BODY WHAT THE
> LEAF IS TO THE WATER. WHAT WOULD ONE BE
> WITHOUT THE OTHER? AS WITH TEA—SO
> WITH LIFE. IS THERE A GREATER UNION?
> —THE MINISTER OF TRAVEL

> "It is proper both for Winter and Summer, preserving in perfect
>   health until extreme old age."
> "It maketh the body active and lusty."
> "It helpeth the Headache, giddiness, and heaviness thereof."
> "It removeth the obstructions of the Spleen."
> "It taketh away the difficulty of breathing, opening obstructions."
> "It is good against Tipitude, Distillations, and cleareth the sight."
> "It removeth lassitude, and cleanseth and purifieth acrid humours,
>   and a hot liver."
> "It is good against crudities, strengthening the weakness of the
>   ventricle or stomach, causing good appetite and digestion, es-
>   pecially for persons of corpulent body, and such as are great
>   eaters of flesh."
> "It vanquisheth heavy dreams, easeth the frame, and strength-
>   eneth the memory."
> "It prevents and cures agues, surfits, and fevers."
> "It strengtheneth the inward parts, and prevents consumption."
> "It is good for colds, dropsys and scurvys; purging the body by
>   sweath, and expelleth infection."
> —"The Qualities of Tea," broadside published in England c. 1660

To understand tea's health benefits, it helps to understand a little about tea's chemistry.

Antioxidants in Tea

Although tea contains virtually no calories, it does contain vitamins A, C, and E, as well as important health-promoting compounds called flavonoids. The flavonoids in tea, called polyphenols, act as antioxidants, countering the effects of reactive oxygen molecules that result from normal body functions and contribute to aging and chronic disease.

One subgroup of polyphenols, the catechins, is abundant in green tea—especially in tea made from the very top of the bush. Catechins were discovered in the 1970s, when medical researchers were looking for the reason people in Japan's Shizuoka Prefecture—a major tea-growing area—had much lower rates of cancer than other Japanese, even when they were heavy smokers. One catechin in particular, epigallocatechin gallate (EGCg), is found in no plant other than tea, and it's one of the most potent antioxidants yet discovered—up to twenty times stronger than vitamin E. Numerous studies have found EGCg to be effective in preventing and inhibiting cancer growth.

Catechins make up as much as 30 percent of the dry weight of green tea leaves, but only three to ten percent of black tea. Steeping the leaves for three to five minutes releases the optimal amount of catechins.

Caffeine in Tea

Caffeine occurs naturally in tea, although in smaller proportions than in coffee, chocolate, or cola drinks. Caffeine is what accounts for tea's reputation as the banisher of fatigue and lifter of spirits. It acts as a stimulant on the central nervous system and the heart, and may increase stomach acid secretion and frequency of urination.

The more oxidized (or "fermented") the tea, the more caffeine it contains: Black tea has the most caffeine, and green tea the least. On average, a six-ounce cup of tea has about 40 milligrams of caffeine—less than half the amount in a cup of brewed coffee. The greatest concentration of caffeine, as with catechins, is in the bud and first two leaves of the tea bush.

Many factors influence the amount of caffeine in a given tea plant: altitude (higher-grown teas tend to have more caffeine), fertilizers, and zinc in the soil are a few of the most important.

Scientific studies of caffeine have been contradictory, but there is no conclusive evidence that caffeine causes or exacerbates any specific illness or medical condition.

Caffeine in Beverages

Most doctors recommend no more than
200 mg of caffeine per day.

Beverage	*Caffeine (mg)*
Coffee (5 ounces)	
Drip method	115
Percolated	80
Instant	65
Decaffeinated	3
Espresso (2 ounces)	60-90
Green tea (5 ounces, brewed 3 minutes)	15
Black tea (5 ounces)	
Brewed 3 minutes	40
Decaffeinated	5
Iced (12 ounces)	70
Cocoa (5 ounces)	4

Chocolate milk (8 ounces)	5
Soft Drinks (12 ounces)	
Coca-Cola	46
Diet Coke	46
Pepsi-Cola	38
Diet Pepsi	40
RC Cola	36
Mountain Dew	54

Source: Food and Drug Administration / National Soft Drink Association

Tea and Cancer

Can tea prevent cancer? That's the question many scientists around the world have been investigating since the 1980s. The catechins in tea are antioxidants, and antioxidants have been shown to prevent the growth of tumors, at least in the laboratory. And there has been some promising evidence that suggests that tea—especially green tea—may protect against certain kinds of cancer.

- A Japanese study published in 1988 found that people who drank ten or more cups of green tea per day had a decreased risk of stomach cancer.
- At least two studies published in the 1990s linked increased consumption of green tea to lower incidences of pancreatic cancer.
- A study published in *Cancer Letters* in 1998 identified ECGg, the catechin in green tea, as the active component inhibiting the growth of

81

human prostate cancer cells *in vitro* (in test tubes).

※ A series of Japanese studies published in 1997, 1998, and 1999 found that ECGg and other green tea polyphenols inhibited the growth of various types of human cancer cells, including colorectal adenocarcinoma, breast ductal cancer, skin cancer, and lung cancer.

※ A study of 35,000 postmenopausal women found that drinking at least two cups of tea daily reduced the risk of digestive and urinary-tract cancers.

※ An article published in the journal *Nature* in 1997, "Why Drinking Tea Could Prevent Cancer," suggested that green tea's antitumor activity derives from its ability to inhibit urokinase (uPA), an enzyme that human cancers use to metastasize. The authors of the article looked at 190,000 compounds known to inhibit uPA—including EGCg. Their conclusion: A single cup of green tea contains more than seven times the concentration of EGCg than the maximum allowable dose of a known uPA inhibitor called amiloride.

There is promising research indicating that tea can prevent cancer as well as inhibit its growth. A study published in a 1999 issue of the journal *Nature*, for example, showed that in *in vitro* (test-tube) tests, EGCg suppressed blood supply to tumors, thus preventing them from growing. Other studies in the late 1990s found that the polyphenols in green tea had preventive effects against prostate cancer and liver cancer.

One study compared the effects of black and green tea infusions on cancer activity. The results, published in 1998 in *Molecular Biology of the Cell*, found that while black tea infusions were effective when diluted in a ten percent solution, green tea infusions were effective in dilutions as low as one percent.

Tea and Heart Disease

There is some evidence that tea protects against heart disease, but the link is not as strong as with cancer. Some lab studies have found that tea polyphenols help lower cholesterol levels and prevent blood clotting, two risk factors in heart disease. Several studies that have looked at human populations have also shown some encouraging results. An Israeli study, for example, found that people who drank black tea had lower cholesterol levels, and coffee drinkers had higher cholesterol levels, than a control group. A study of 20,000 Norwegian men and women, published in 1992, found that those who drank five or more cups of black tea per day had lower levels of cholesterol than those who drank no tea.

One of the largest studies looked at 12,763 middle-aged men from seven countries. Published in 1995, in the *Archives of Internal Medicine*, the "Seven Countries Study" found a strong positive correlation between flavonoid content of the diet and low risk of heart disease. Flavonoids are, of course, abundantly present in tea.

Tea may contribute to a healthy heart by promoting a healthy body weight. A study by Chinese researchers published in 1998 found a significant decrease in the weight of rats after 63 weeks of consuming a mix of their regular feed and powdered green tea leaves; at week 15 the green tea group already weighed 12 percent less than the control group.

And a Dutch study published in 1999 looked at 3,454 people who drank one to two cups of black tea daily and found they had a 46 percent lower risk of severe aortic atherosclerosis, which is a factor in cardiovascular disease. Those who drank more than four cups a day had a 69 percent lower risk.

One phenomenon many scientists have observed is that tea drinkers often have better health habits than the general population. Certainly a sip-by-sip life—relaxed, contemplative, mindful—is less stressful than a gulp-by-gulp life, and perhaps healthier for your heart as well.

Tea and Teeth

That cup of after-dinner green tea does more than soothe your mind and belly: it fights cavities, too.

Tea is rich in fluoride—In fact, fluoride is the only mineral found in significant quantities in tea. And fluoride is known to fight tooth decay: That's the reason it's added to municipal water supplies and to toothpastes and mouthwashes. Fluoridated water usually contains between 0.7 and 1.2 parts per million (ppm), while green tea naturally contains between 1.32 and 4.18 ppm. And there's no danger of fluoride toxicity when you drink tea. (Just don't add any sugar—that would defeat the purpose!)

The benefits of tea on oral health were demonstrated in a Japanese study published in a dental research magazine in 1994. Thirty-five volunteers age 18 to 29 were asked to refrain from brushing or flossing their teeth for four days. Instead, they rinsed their mouths with a solution of tea polyphenols after each meal and before bedtime. In 34 of the volunteers, bacterial counts and plaque were significantly decreased.

Tea has other beneficial effects on oral health. In lab tests, the catechins in all kinds of tea—black, green, Oolong, and pu-erh—have been shown to inhibit or even destroy the bacteria that cause dental plaque. Even a single cup of tea produced this protective effect.

Tea and Bones

Osteoporosis, or brittle-bone disease, is a major health problem for older adults, especially women. Some studies have linked caffeine intake to osteoporosis, so naturally tea drinkers have been concerned. But a study of more than 1,200 British women, published in 2000 in the *American Journal of Clinical Nutrition*, found that tea drinking actually protected against fractures of the hip bones, which are among the most dangerous of all breaks. The women, who were between the ages of 65 and 76, included more than 1,100 tea drinkers. Those who added milk to their tea enjoyed the greatest benefits, probably because of the protective effect of the calcium in the milk.

It's not clear why tea is beneficial to bone mineral density. The fluoride naturally present in tea may play a role, and the study's author suggests that tea may also contain components that weakly mimic the effect of the female hormone estrogen. Estrogen is known to be a protective factor in bone health.

Pu-erh Tea and Health

The class of teas known as Pu-erh have long been drunk in China for their medicinal benefits. Pu-erh tea is customarily drunk with or after meals, especially fatty meals, because of its purported ability to lower cholesterol and to reduce indigestion and diarrhea.

In clinical tests, one green Pu-erh called Tuocha has been shown to cleanse the arteries of the plaque that's a risk factor in heart disease. According to tea writer James Norwood Pratt, for this reason Tuocha now accounts for one-quarter of all the tea drunk in France.

Other Possible Health Benefits of Tea

Antiviral: In lab tests, the catechins in tea leaves have been found to inhibit viral infections such as flu, herpes simplex, and polio virus 1.

Antibacterial: Green tea especially, but also black, Oolong, and pu-erh, have been found to inhibit the growth of *Streptococcus mutans*, a bacterium that acts on sugars in the mouth to produce plaque.

Digestion: For years, mothers have known that the BRAT diet—bananas, rice, applesauce, and tea—is an effective home remedy for diarrhea. Both black tea and green tea have this effect, largely because of their flavonoids.

Immune system: At least two studies in the 1990s found the EGCg, the catechin found only in tea leaves, strengthened the body's immune system by promoting the growth of disease-fighting T-cells and B-cells.

Weight control: The polyphenols in green tea have been shown to inhibit the activity of amylase, an enzyme in saliva that speeds up the digestion of carbohydrates. It's been theorized that because of this, green tea may promote fat burning over fat storage. One small, double-blind study of obese middle-aged women, published in 1985, looked at the effect of green tea capsules as dietary supplements. After two weeks, the green tea group had lost twice as much weight as the group that was given placebos; after four weeks, the green tea group had lost three times as much weight as the controls.

Other Healthy Ways to Enjoy Tea

Black tea has an astringent and mildly disinfecting effect on the skin, making it an ideal topical remedy for inflammations. Cool, wet tea bags applied to the skin can soothe burns and rashes; applied to closed eyes, they can reduce puffiness. Adding a quart of strong black tea to lukewarm bath water can take the sting out of sunburn.

Green tea extract is being added to many cosmetics because of its antioxidant effect. It may or may not combat the aging process, as manufacturers claim, but it does act as a natural preservative to keep face creams and lotions fresh longer.

For sore, aching feet, add leftover tea bags to a warm footbath.

Adding tea to rinsewater after your shampoo will soften hair and enhance its sheen.

Of course, one of the healthiest aspects of tea is its encouragement of a slowed-down sip-by-sip life, one that allows for social interaction and personal reflection; a life of attention, balance, and well-being. You will laugh more. You will look at your watch less. You will have fewer imaginary problems, once you have learned to sip. In our fast paced, hurried world, that may be the best "medicine" of all!

chapter 5.

A GLOSSARY
OF TEA

T HOUGH THIS IS but an introduction to the vast
world of tea varietals, we hope it will inspire you
to sample some of the many fine teas available to
the seeker of TeaMind.

Please note that the descriptions and tasting notes
herein apply to the finest grades of each varietal, and
may not be suitable for lower grades that sometimes
masquerade as the genuine article. Higher-grade teas
lack bitterness even after being infused for five minutes
or longer; they also tend to bear premium price tags.

Because tea is a natural product, even the highest
grades may vary in taste depending on their freshness
and on the weather, soil conditions, and elevation
where they were grown.

Black Teas

Assam (India) ah-SAHM: One of the world's most popular teas, and often among the best. Grown in the low-lying Assam region of northeastern India, it's typically astringent, robust, and "malty," with  an orange or red liquor; it's often mixed into "breakfast" blends, and is well suited to the addition of milk and sugar. Noteworthy Assam gardens include Thowra, Numalighur, Paneery, Booteachang, Nudwa, and Jayshree; all produce teas by the time-consuming orthodox method.

Ceylon (Sri Lanka) say-LAWN: Encompasses both CTC and orthodox teas that may be high-, medium-, or low-grown. The low-grown leaves tend to be cultivated for quantity, while the high-grown tea may be spectacular, with a very black leaf that yields a rich, mellow, reddish-brown infusion—lighter in character than Assam and not as flowery as Darjeeling. In general, Ceylon teas are known for their "brightness," "liveliness," and blendability. Teas grown in the Uva district, between 4,000 and 6,000 feet on the eastern slops of the island's central mountains, are acclaimed for their special mellowness. Other important districts include Dimbula and Nuwara, whose teas are often blended with fruits and essential oils. Blends advertised as "Orange pekoe" often include Ceylon.

Darjeeling (India) dar-JEE-ling: Exquisite small-leafed varietal grown in the foothills of the Himalayas ("Darjeeling" means "Land of the Thunderbolt"); it's known for its clarity, light but flavorful cup, and complex characteristics—including a distinctive "Muscat" aroma. Darjeeling teas are always produced by the orthodox method, and leaves are intentionally broken during manufacture.  The closely planted Darjeeling gardens roll up the mountainsides from 3,000 to 6,000 feet; the higher elevations yield lighter, more flowery teas.

Similar to wine, Darjeelings are sometimes identified and sold by estate (the plantation where the leaves were grown, such as Glenburn, Bloomfield, Namring, or Castleton) and by flush:

- ❦ **First flush (April/May):** Plucked from the first growth; light and flowery
- ❦ **Second flush (May/June):** Harvested from the second growth; fruitier and smoother
- ❦ **Autumnal flush (Timing depends on when monsoon rainfall occurs):** Larger-leafed, harvested after the rainy season; "rounder" in taste.

Darjeeling teas are scarce and expensive, and are rarely sold unblended. When the leaves come from a single harvest and are unblended, it is called vintage. Some store-bought "Darjeelings" may contain only 50 percent Darjeeling leaves.

Dooars or *Duars* (India) DOO-arz: Tea from a small, low-lying district between Darjeeling and Assam; its flavor is less potent than Assam's. Used mostly in blends.

Keemun or *Qimen* (China) KEY-min: China's most celebrated black tea, grown in Anhwei (or Anhui) province in east-central China. Keemun is a subvariety of tea, rather than simply a style; it's the only tea leaf that contains myrcenal, an essential oil that gives Keemun its sweetness (described by one rhapsodic chronicler as "like a dying black rose") and its nearly unique ability to gain rather than lose character as it ages. Fine Keemun has a small, slender, tightly curled, very black leaf; the infusion is sweet with suggestions of apple and plum, a bit smoky, and well bodied. Often enjoyed, by itself or in blends, as a breakfast tea. The absolute finest grade of Keemun, which is not necessarily produced each year because of seasonal variations, is Hao Ya.

Nilgiri (southern India) nil-GEAR-ee: From the Tamil word for "Blue Mountains," a hilly region at the southernmost tip of India, close to Sri Lanka. High-grown Nilgiris combine the flavor of Ceylon teas with the body of India teas: clean, well balanced, and slightly lemony. In India, Nilgiri is often used as the base for chai—the spicy, milky tea blend enjoyed by millions of Indians. Although it is generally blended, the Indian Tea Board considers it a "self drinker," meaning that it is worth drinking unblended. Nilgiri shares this distinction with Darjeeling and Assam teas.

North China Congou (China) con-GOO: "Congou" is a corruption of *gongfu*, which means (roughly) "skill and practice." It was the name by which Europeans first knew China black tea, and it's still used as a generic trade name. North China's most famous Congou teas include Keemun, Ningchow, and Ichang; the Chinese know them as "black-leaf" teas, as opposed to South China's "red-leaf" teas.

Sikkim (India) SIK-im: Grown near Darjeeling, it is less well known and therefore not as expensive. It has a malty yet delicate flavor.

South China Congou (China) con-GOO: See *North China Congou*. South China's most famous Congou teas include Paklum, Panyong, Pakling, Padrae, and Yunnan.

Yunnan (China) YOU-nahn: Tea grown in a mountainous southwestern China province since ancient times. Production of black tea from this varietal, however, began only in 1939. It is easy to identify by its thick, broad, soft leaves and fat leaf buds (tip) that can lend it a golden or khaki color. Yunnan has an assertive, peppery flavor that makes it an excellent brown breakfast brew. It's also used in scented blends and as a base for fine iced tea. It is also sometimes used in Russian Caravan blends.

Black Tea Blends

English Breakfast: Originally not a blend at all, but rather straight Keemun, it was given its name by British tea marketers. Today the term may apply to any combination of China, Ceylon, and India teas that yields a brew with medium body and brisk character. Usually drunk with milk.

Irish Breakfast: Another marketing term. Heartier than English Breakfast, it's usually made from high-grown Ceylon and robust Assam. Also good with milk.

Russian Caravan: Originally, Russian tea was brick tea imported from China by caravan; along the way, the leaves picked up the aroma of campfire smoke. Today the blend is likely to be made from China and Formosa Oolongs, unspecified black teas, and Lapsang Souchong. The blend is then cured with smoke to give it its characteristic aroma and flavor.

I AM TOLD THAT IN WESTERN CULTURES THERE IS A PREOCCUPATION WITH YOUTH BUT THAT YOU HAVE NOT YET DISCOVERED THE INSPIRING EFFECTS OF TeaMind. HOW CAN IT BE? A SINGLE SIP OF TEA HAS THE POWER TO CARRY YOU BACK TO THE TIME BEFORE TIME. NOW THAT'S YOUNG.
—THE MINISTER OF LEAVES

Flavored and Scented Black Teas

Earl Grey: Said to be the first scented tea drunk in the West. It's made of China black, Ceylon, or India tea scented with oil of bergamot, extracted from a small citrus fruit grown in the Mediterranean and sprayed on the leaves after manufacture. There are many grades of bergamot oil, some natural, some synthetic. The best Earl Grey balances a natural orangey flavor with the tea taste, without one overwhelming the other. Attributed, probably apocryphally, to the British Earl Grey, who visited China in 1830.

Lapsang Souchong (China) LAP-sang SOO-shong: Grown in China but rarely drunk there, this tea is immediately identifiable by its smoky aroma, obtained from curing in smoke-filled rooms (like ham) over pine needles. It is often found in Russian Caravan teas, and the leaf yields a dark-red infusion that goes especially well with savory dishes.

Chai: The Indian word for "tea" and the ubiquitous brew of India, made from a combination of black (or, sometimes, green) tea leaves and a combination of spices. Quality can range from very pleasant to dreadful. Milk (often evaporated or condensed) is usually added.

Fruit-blended Teas

For centuries, fruit trees have been planted in tea gardens to shade the growing tea bushes. When breezes blew, the fragrant flowers drifted over the tea leaves and dusted them with pollen and petals. The tradition of combining fruit, flowers, and tea continues to this day. In China, the sweet-tart lichee fruit is used to flavor black tea; in

Lichee fruit

India, dried mangoes may be added to Assam leaves. Oranges, plums, and tropical fruits such as papaya are sometimes blended with tea and spices, and rose and cherry blossoms lend their sweet fragrance to some delicious blended teas.

Oolong Teas

Formosa Oolong (Taiwan): Preferred by connoisseurs all over the world, Formosa oolong is categorized by grades (Standard is the lowest grade, followed in ascending order by Choice, Choicest, Fancy, and Fanciest). The top grades may cost as much as ten times more than other top-grade teas. Dry leaves are large and lightly- to well-rolled, with an abundance of silver tips; infused leaves are rusty brown and very large. Highly aromatic and completely lacking in astringency, the tea has a flower upper register and a flavor compared to chestnut, honey, and peaches.

Pouchong (Taiwan) POO-chong: A lightly oxidized, partially rolled oolong used as a base for the best jasmine tea.

Ti Kuan Yin ("Iron Goddess of Mercy") (China) tee quawn YIN: Named for a Buddhist goddess, this tea comes from Northern Fujian, in mainland China. The most revered of Chinese Oolongs, it has tightly twisted, shiny dark leaves and a strong peachy flavor that is somewhat more astringent than Oolongs from Taiwan. It can be infused more than once—up to seven times, as lore has it—and is known for its digestive properties.

Wuyi (China) woo-YEE: A large category of Chinese Oolong teas, said to have originated in the Wuyi Mountains along the western border of Fujian province and exported since the eighteenth cen- tury. Europeans first knew this tea as "Bohea." Upon immersion, the large, crinkled leaves become bright green in their centers and slowly turn red around the edges.

Green Teas

Bancha (Japan) BAHN-cha: Literally "last tea," bancha is made from coarse late-harvested leaves. It is drunk in Japan as everyday tea, and is not much exported.

Baozhong or *Bao Jong* or *Pouchong* (China): Withered before firing, its taste falls somewhere in between green tea and Oolong. It is often used to make Jasmine tea.

Dragonwell (Long Jing, Lung Ching) (China): One of China's most celebrated teas, it has four unique characteristics: light jade-green color, lingering mellow taste, expansive earthy aroma, and a long, flat shape. The best Dragonwell is plucked "before the rains"—traditionally, before early April—and made completely by hand; it is recognized by its bright and shiny hand-flattened leaf. It requires cooler water than most green teas; some experts say it can be made with lukewarm water. It has a cooling effect when drunk in hot weather.

Gen Mai Cha (Japan) Ghen my CHA: A Japanese specialty: green sencha tea leaves blended with fire-toasted rice. A hearty tea, originally made by peasants unable to afford straight tea, it has a slightly salty, grainy taste that is filling as well as quenching. Finer grades have a natural sweetness to the finish. Sometimes called "popcorn" tea—the rice sometimes pops open during shipping.

Gu Zhang Mao Jian (China) Goo shong mao chee-ON: Tender, silver-tipped leaves are harvested for only ten days each spring on the banks of the Quishui River in the Wuyi Mountains. Although it is a green tea, it is very slightly oxidized to give the dry leaves a dark cast. The taste is much smoother than many traditional Chinese green teas, with a faint sweetness and unique chestnut character.

Gunpowder (China, Taiwan): Said to have been given its name by a British East India Company agent in China who thought the tiny, tightly rolled pellets resembled buckshot. The Chinese call it "Pearl Tea." Each leaf is rolled into a ball that "explodes" when infused with hot water. Fine gunpowder has a yellow-green liquor and a penetrating, refreshing taste. Formosan gunpowder is notably lighter and sweeter than Chinese. In Morocco, it's used to make mint tea.

Gyokuro (Japan) ghee-OH-koo-roe: Literally "Pearl Dew," this is the finest grade of tea exported from Japan.

It is produced by shielding the tea bushes while the first flush develops; deprived of sun, the leaves develop extra chlorophyll (making them dark green) and fewer polyphenols, resulting in a mild, sweet taste. The manufactured tea has flat, sharply pointed leaves like pine needles; liquor is distinctly green, sweet, and smooth-tasting—a very refined tea for special occasions. One basket-fired variety is called "Spider Leg."

Hojicha (Japan) HO-ji-cha: Bancha tea leaves that are oven roasted after manufacture to produce an earthy aroma and nutty flavor. The liquor is light brown, with a robust greeting and subtle finish. Low in caffeine, this tea is said to have restorative qualities.

Hyson (China) HIGH-sun: A type of tea made from wild tea trees in west-central Zhejiang Province. The leaves are thick and yellow-green and are twisted long and thin during manufacture. Called Chunmee ("Precious Eyebrow") in Chinese, Hyson got its name from the similarity between the term yu-tsien ("before the rains," referring to the best grade of tea) to the name of an eighteenth-century tea merchant, one Philip Hyson. In China, Hyson tea is ordinary, everyday green tea.

Longjing or *Lung Ching* (China) LONG-jing: Literally "Dragon Well," this tea is named for a well which was said to be inhabited by a dragon. It is a complex and subtle tea, with a slightly sweet flavor.

Matcha (Japan) MA-cha: A powdered leaf traditionally used in the Japanese tea ceremony. It is whisked with boiling water in a bowl to create a frothy, bright-green, nourishing beverage (like all Japanese teas, matcha is high in vitamin C). The finest grades are sweet and smooth. Before it is powdered, it is called Tencha.

Pi Lo Chun (China) pee low CHUN: Also called Biluochun, Green Snail Spring, or Astounding Fragrance, this is a rare and famous tea that is processed completely by hand. Peach, apricot, and plum trees are planted amid the tea bushes and are in full bloom when the tender new tea leaves unfold, so that they impart their fragrance to the lucky person who drinks the tea. Pi Lo Chun is so delicate that it must be steeped in water of only 175°F; the leaves are added to the hot water instead of the other way round.

Sencha (Japan) SEN-cha: A general term for the "ordinary" tea of Japan, although it can also apply to some excellent and expensive teas. It can be processed in many ways: pan-fired, basket-fired, natural, or "guri" (curled).

DAY AFTER DAY WE LIVE ON THE EDGE OF TIME.
SUN AND MOON GO AS THEY MAY. HEAVEN
AND EARTH CHANGE FREELY.
WITH EACH CUP OF TEA I EXPERIENCE THE
BIRTH OF THE UNIVERSE.
WITH EACH SIP A NEW BEGINNING.
IF YOU ASK ME TO EXPLAIN, I NEED ONLY
INVITE YOU TO DRINK THE TEA.
—THE MINISTER OF TRAVEL

Green Tea Blends

Jasmine tea: What Earl Grey is to the West, jasmine tea is to North China. The jasmine plant was brought to China from Persia before the third century A.D., and its flowers began appearing in tea around the fifth century. The night-blooming flowers are picked in the morning and kept in a cool place till nightfall. Just as they are about to open, they are piled next to heat-dried green tea leaves (or Oolong), which absorb the jasmine fragrance. The process is repeated two or three times for ordinary jasmine tea, and up to seven times for top grades like Yin Hao. Jasmine Pearls are hand-rolled pellets that "explode" in hot water, releasing their intoxicating perfume. Beware inferior jasmine teas that are artificially scented with extracts and oils. Note, too, that the presence of flowers in the loose tea has no bearing on its quality; some excellent jasmine teas contain no blossoms at all. Jasmine tea contains antioxidants and vitamin C, and soothes the digestive system.

Green chai: Although traditional chai is made with black tea leaves, recently green tea chai blends have been introduced. Care must be taken to avoid overwhelming the more delicate flavors of green tea with spices and fruit flavors.

Fruit teas: Cherry, apple, and orange are a few of the fruit flavors that can be successfully blended with green tea. Fruit essences and aromatic blossoms such as hibiscus and rose are sometimes added for flavor and appearance.

Pu-erh Tea

Pu-erh (China) poo-AIR: A broad category of teas produced in Yunnan province from a large-leafed variety of *Camellia sinensis*. After harvesting and initial firing, the moist tea is heaped into large piles, where a natural bacterium creates a chemical reaction. The pile is carefully turned to maintain the proper balance of temperature and moisture. There are green (unoxidized) and black (oxidized) pu-erhs; both tend to have bold, earthy flavors that first-time tasters either love or hate. Research has shown that pu-erh cleanses the arteries of plaque, and assists in weight control.

White Tea

Pai Mu Tan (China) pie moo TAHN: Also called "White Peony." White tea is truly rare and produced only in China. It is neither rolled nor oxidized, only steamed, and is made from buds of a special bush known as "Big White," sometimes blended with buds of the Shui Hsien plant. Because it is 100 percent tip, this is the most tender and delicate cup available. Infuse it with water significantly cooler than boiling, preferably between 170° and 185°F.

Part Two

HERBS

AN HERB IS A FRIEND.
IT SHOULD BE CHOSEN WISELY
AND ENTERTAINED DISCRIMINATELY.
—THE MINISTER OF HERBS

chapter 6.

HERBS AND HERBAL "TEAS"

What Is an Herb?

ANY INTRODUCTION to herbs must begin with this riddle: What is an herb?

The classical definition of an herb is "a plant that lacks a woody stem and that dies back in winter." Concise, but not really an accurate description of many of the plants we use to make tea. Some of the most important ones, such as Siberian ginseng, cinnamon, and lemon, definitely have woody stems.

Let's try again. An herb is sometimes defined as "any plant whose leaves, stems, and flowers have aromatic or medicinal properties." This is closer. Yet some flowers or flower parts—such as saffron or vanilla—are called spices rather than herbs. And

Garlic bulb

sometimes an herb is a root (licorice, ginger), a bulb (garlic), a seed (anise), or a fruit (black currant, elderberry). Some herbs are vines; others are shrubs. In all, there are probably more than 10,000 species of "herbs" around the world.

So here is a more practical definition: Herbs are plants or plant parts that are used in fresh, dried, or extracted form to lift our spirits, season our food, dye our fabrics, heal our ailments, and mend our wounds.

What Makes an Herb?

Plant parts used to create familiar herbs

Bark: Cassia, cinnamon, pau d'arco
Bulb: Garlic
Flowers: Chamomile, echinacea, lavender, saffron, vanilla
Fruit: Black currant, elderberry, hawthorn berry
Leaves: Echinacea, mints, rooibos, yerba maté, rosemary, sage, skullcap, thyme
Root: Astragalus, echinacea, ginger, ginseng, licorice, valerian
Seeds: Anise, dill, echinacea

Of course, not all herbs are congenial. Nature's harvest includes many forms of poison, from mildly sedative to dramatically fatal. Hemlock, henbane, mandrake, and belladonna were once called "witches' herbs" for

106

Mandrake root

their power to paralyze and kill. Other herbs may produce welcome or unwelcome sedative, laxative, or diuretic effects. And some herbs, such as digitalis (foxglove), are safe only when carefully prepared as medication and administered by a medical professional. The humblest plants often are the most benign, while the showiest are sometimes the most dangerous.

It should also be noted that several herbs—among them maté, guaraná, cola nuts, ephedra, and gota kola—contain caffeine or other stimulants. If you choose an herbal infusion as a caffeine-free alternative to tea, coffee, or cocoa, you should read the label carefully to make sure your selection in fact contains no stimulants.

Where Are Herbs Grown?

Herbs are harvested in virtually every corner of the globe. In the wild, herbs are native to deserts, mountains, the tropics, and the temperate regions. Some herbs—the seaweeds—are even harvested from the oceans.

Many herbs are cultivated herbs; others are gathered from the wild, or "wildcrafted" (see below).

What's in an Herb?

Every herb is a complex of substances, some active, others inert or neutral. The inert substances often work in synergy with the active elements to speed up or slow down their absorption in the body. That's why the drugs isolated from plants usually work quite differently from the intact whole plant.

The amount and strength of an herb's active substances can vary depending on the soil in which it was grown, the harvesting method, and the preparation technique. Good-quality herbs are desirable because they're consistent.

Active substances in herbs may include:

Bitters: Bitter constituents, called Amara, stimulate the secretion of gastric juices and have a tonic effect on the body as a whole. Herbs that contain bitters do not necessarily taste particularly bitter; ginger, for example, contains bitter constituents, *Amara acria*, that are acrid in character.

Essential oils: Most plants contain essential oils, which are volatile and usually unpleasant in odor. The essential oils are stored in a plant's oil cells, ducts, or glandular hairs. They are very complex, consisting of as many as 100 substances. Essential oils often have an anti-inflammatory effect on the body.

Flavonoids: This broad category of substances is present in many plants, including tea (*Camellia sinensis*) and many herbs. Depending on their type and amount in a plant, flavonoids can have a variety of effects on the body. In tea, they act as antioxidants, repairing damage to cells. In general, flavonoids aid digestion and affect the cardiovascular system.

Polyphenols: Herbs that contain a high proportion

of polyphenols—for example, strawberry leaves, rooibos, and the mints—have an astringent and antibacterial quality.

Glycosides: Glycosides are present in many herbs,
and have widely differing effects on the body. Some act
as cardiac stimulants, others as laxatives, and still others
as sudorifics (tending to cause sweat).

Saponins: The root of this word means "soap":
saponins produce froth and foam and emulsify oil in
water. They are useful in breaking up congestion and
stubborn coughs, and often have a diuretic effect.
Licorice and calendula (pot marigolds) are examples of
herbs in which saponin is a primary active ingredient.

Mucilage: Mucilage is the carbohydrate-containing
substance in plants that swells on contact with water.
Plants with a high proportion of mucilage, such as
marshmallow, have a soothing effect on the body. Mucilage also moderates the tart flavor of certain plants
such as raspberries.

Vitamins and minerals: All vegetables, herbs included, are important sources of nutrients in the human
diet. Some herbs are notable for their high proportion
of a specific vitamin or mineral: For example, rose hips
contain large quantities of vitamin C; hibiscus contains
the minerals calcium, niacin, riboflavin, and iron.

Herbal Products

Herbs can be prepared in many ways for human consumption. The familiar culinary herbs—basil, oregano,

parsley, and so on—are often enjoyed fresh. Other herbs are usually dried, and sometimes powdered, before being made into capsules, pills, or liquid products.

There are several categories of liquid herbal preparations:

Infusions, or *tisanes* in French, are beverages made by steeping dried or fresh plant parts in water that has come to a boil.

Decoctions, used widely in Asia for medicinal purposes, are made by boiling the plant parts in water until the liquid is reduced. The water is then strained into a cup or teapot.

Aqueous extracts are concentrated preparations made by evaporating the water in which a plant has been boiled.

Alcohol extracts are made by steeping herbs in alcohol or a mixture of alcohol and water. The herbs steep for at least two weeks, and the solution is shaken daily. Usually sold in dropper bottles, alcohol extracts (also called **tinctures**) should be labeled with a ratio indicating the proportion of herb to liquid. If one kilogram of herb is extracted to create one kilogram of extract, the result is "1:1" preparation.

Standardized extracts are made under scientific examination; every dose of the extract is determined to contain the same level of a specific compound naturally found within the herb. Standardized extracts are often used for creating tablets or capsules used as remedies. Both aqueous and alcohol extracts can be standardized.

Standardization helps consumers compare the strength of different companies' products.

Cultivating Herbs

Every common herb, and some not-so-common ones, grew wild at one time in the past. Some still do. (And some only seem to, as any backyard gardener who has tried to clear out a mint patch or blackberry bramble will attest.)

Today, the herbs used in herbal tea are usually grown in one of three ways: from a windowsill or backyard garden, from a commercial plot, or collected in the wild ("wildcrafted").

Different herbs require widely varying growing conditions and cultivation techniques. For that reason, many commercial growers specialize in a particular crop.

Organic Herbs

The rise of organic farming is one of the most encouraging trends in herb cultivation. Certified organic herbs are grown without synthetic chemicals or pesticides, relying instead on sustainable agricultural methods that respect the health of the soil and the people who cultivate it. Organic herbs command a higher price that corresponds to the extra care needed to farm in this way.

Wildcrafted Herbs

Most commercial herbs are cultivated, but some—for example, saw palmetto and rosehips—are picked from the wild or "wildcrafted." Although wildcrafting sounds romantic and "natural," in fact it is a controversial practice. Wildcrafting has endangered several North American wild plants, including wild American ginseng (native to Wisconsin) and goldenseal. Echinacea, once wildcrafted almost to extinction, is making a comeback in the wild because of extensive cultivation efforts.

Some herbalists say wildcrafted herbs are the most potent, medicinally speaking, and the purest because they have been taken from their natural habitat. On the other hand, care must be taken not to wildcraft plants that do not regenerate easily.

Cultivated herbs are sometimes more consistent in flavor, appearance, and potency. And cultivating herbs instead of wildcrafting them has another benefit: It provides a sustainable way of life for farmers and keeps agricultural land in productive use.

112

chapter 7.

ENJOYING HERBS

ERBS HAVE BEEN savored as foods and flavorings for at least as long as they've been appreciated medicinally. Herbal infusions have probably been around for as long as humans have known how to boil water.

Over the centuries, through countless experiments, people have found ways to derive the most pleasure and benefit from herbs. Usually that meant blending them: Although some people prefer a single herb's flavor by itself, most enjoy the synergistic effect of several in a blend.

What Is Herb Tea?

Strictly speaking, "tea" refers only to beverages made from the leaves of the *Camellia sinensis* bush—the plant that gives us black, green, and Oolong tea. Beverages made from other plants are often called "infusions" (their common name in England). In France, herbal "teas" are called "tisanes."

In these pages, we use "herbal infusion" and "herb tea" interchangeably.

Hibiscus

Simples and Blends

The first herb teas were almost certainly made from one herb at a time. A single herb was known as a "simple," and the process of experimenting with it was called simpling. Simpling is still the best way to appreciate the flavor and effect of each herb and to understand how blending enhances them.

Some herbs, such as chamomile or peppermint, are frequently enjoyed in their unblended form. Many others, such as ginseng or valerian, have a bitter or even unpleasant taste best disguised by the addition of other herbs and spices. Certain combinations blend so happily that they are classics: linden blossoms and peppermint; rose hips and hibiscus.

Herbs Plus Tea

Besides being blended with one another, herbs can also be blended with black, green, or Oolong tea (*Camellia sinensis*). These blends bring together new and familiar flavors in healthful, delicious combinations.

How to Brew Herbs

Brewing a delicious herbal infusion is blissfully easy:

1. Boil water: Fill a kettle with water and bring it to the boil.
2. Infuse herbs: Cover herbs with just-boiled water and allow to steep.
3. Drink infusion: If you like, add lemon, honey, or sugar to taste.

A few guidelines can help you derive the most pleasure from your herbal brew:

Use fresh cold water. As with black, green, or Oolong tea, the purer and better-tasting the water, the more satisfying the results. If your tap water has an off taste, experiment with filtered and bottled waters.

Use full-leaf herbs when possible. The more intact the leaf or flower, the better its essences are preserved. When herbs are finely pulverized, their greater surface area allows their essential oils (responsible for fragrance

115

and taste) to evaporate quickly. Infusers (see below) are almost as easy to use as tea bags.

Use proper equipment. Herbs need space and good water circulation to unfold and release their flavors into the water. For infusing, choose a bamboo, plastic, or wire mesh basket that can be dipped into a single cup. For making larger quantities, use a teapot with a built-in mesh infuser. Perforated stainless-steel tea balls or spoons are a last resort: They limit water flow and reduce the amount of space needed for herbs to expand.

Your cup and teapot should be made of glass or ceramic; metal can impart a metallic flavor to the herbs, and may even leach undesirable minerals into the infusion. Warm the teapot and cup by swirling some steaming-hot water in it, and then pour it out.

How much herb? Experiment! Herbs are more forgiving than black or green tea; if you make an infusion that's too strong, you can always dilute it with a little more hot water. A good starting point is one rounded teaspoon of dried herb per cup—one and a half to two grams.

How hot? Allow the water to come to a full boil, then turn off the heat. Pour the hot water immediately over the herbs. Unlike black or green tea, the water does not need to cool off.

How long to steep? Herbs should be brewed a little longer than black tea, and considerably longer than green tea. About five minutes is a good rule of thumb—more or less depending on your preference. Blends made with roots and barks may require a little more time.

116

When you first sample a new herb or blend, taste it at intervals to determine what strength you prefer.

Remove the herbs or strain off the liquid when the tea reaches the desired strength. Most herbs should not be infused more than once. Used, wet herbs make a fine mulch and fertilizer in your garden or compost pile.

Drinking tea. A well-balanced herbal infusion is delicious without any additions. But depending on your preference, you may want to add sugar, honey, or lemon to your cup. Some robust herbal infusions, such as those made with rooibos, chicory, or yerba maté, benefit from the addition of a bit of warm or steamed milk.

Herbal Sun Tea

On a warm, sunny day, you can make herbal infusions with solar power. Place herbs and fresh water in a clear glass jar and set it in the sun. Check the strength occasionally; when it is to your taste, strain off the liquid and enjoy.

Making Iced Herbal Tea

An iced tea pitcher—tall, with a removable infusing basket—is a convenience for making refreshing iced herbal teas. Place the herbs in the basket and pour just-boiled water over them. When the infusion reaches the desired strength, remove the basket and place the pitcher in the refrigerator to chill. Or pour the hot infusion over a tall glass filled with ice cubes.

Tasting Herbal Infusions

How should you evaluate your herbal infusion? With black or green tea, there's an agreed-upon tasting vocabulary. Not so with herbal teas: Every herb, every blend, and every cup is likely to be different from the last. Here are a few guidelines that may be helpful; you may want to add some of your own.

Body: The body of the tea is the base that carries the flavor notes. A well-formulated herbal tea has a strong body (not to be confused with dark color) that lends a deep and full dimension to the beverage. Flat, weak, and watery teas are undesirable.

Color: Depending on the dominant herb, herbal infusions can be almost any color from light yellow-green (desirable in chamomile tea) to golden (characteristic of teas made with cinnamon or cardamom) to deep brown (as with chicory and carob teas) to bright red (hibiscus tea). The color should be appealing and have pleasant associations with the flavor, body, and fragrance of the beverage. Some people like to match their tea to the season, preferring lighter colors in summer and darker colors in autumn and winter.

Flavor: A well-blended herbal tea has a full complement of flavors with base, middle, and top notes—not unlike fine perfume. No single flavor should overwhelm the others. With practice, you may be able to distinguish three or four flavor notes—green, flowery, fruity, spicy, rooty, and so on.

The Five Flavors

Classical Chinese medicine recognizes five elements—wood, fire, earth, metal, and water—each of which has a corresponding flavor. A balanced diet carefully combines the flavors and calibrates them to the needs of the individual.

The five flavors are:

Sour—corresponds to wood. Sour herbs such as hibiscus have an astringent quality.

Bitter—corresponds to fire. Bitter herbs include lavender, skullcap, valerian, and chamomile; they are believed to have a cooling effect.

Sweet—corresponds to earth. Licorice, stevia, and Chinese sweet blackberry leaves are classified as sweet herbs; they are considered tonic and nutritious.

Pungent—corresponds to metal. Pungent herbs such as ginger, cinnamon, and thyme are believed to affect lungs and large intestine.

Salty—corresponds to water. The seaweeds are characterized by their saltiness, and are considered "cooling."

One herb, schizandra—*wu wei zi* in Chinese—is known as "Five Taste Fruit" because it combines all five flavors.

Natural vs. Artificial Flavoring

Herbal blends are often enhanced by flavors that balance the herbs' natural taste or mask an innate bitterness common to many herbs. Many natural flavors used in herbal teas to enhance their flavor come from the essential oils or flavor components of the herbs themselves. For instance, wintergreen leaves are often enhanced with wintergreen oil. Other flavors like citrus or vanilla come from extracts and oils derived from fruits or spices. By law, such enhancements have to be labeled either "natural" or "artificial"; artificial flavors are made using chemicals compounded in laboratories.

> **Natural flavoring:** *The essential oil or other extract of a spice, fruit, vegetable, edible yeast, herb, bark, bud, root, leaf, meat, seafood, poultry, eggs, or dairy product, whose significant function in food is flavoring rather than nutritional.*
>
> **Artificial flavoring:** *Any substance used to impart flavor to food that is not derived from the above list.*
>
> *Source: U.S. Food and Drug Administration*

Other Ways to Enjoy Herbs

Herbs have a long history of use as cosmetics and skin treatments. Here are just a few of the traditional ways in which herbs can make life more beautiful or relaxing.

Bath: Add a rooibos infusion to bathwater to relieve itching, rashes, and sunburn. Brew a pot of lavender tea and add it to your bath water for a fragrant soak. A pot of strong valerian tea added to bathwater is said to be a sleep aid.

Hair: An infusion of rosemary leaves is said to be a remedy for dandruff. Sage tea is reputed to restore color to gray hair; chamomile tea is recommended for bringing out golden highlights in blonde hair.

Skin: A compress made from an infusion of lemon balm is said to relieve painful swelling. A raspberry-leaf infusion was traditionally used to bathe wounds. Add essential oil of nutmeg, thyme, or rosemary to almond oil for an aromatic and soothing massage oil.

Eyes: Cool, damp tea bags filled with elder flowers or eyebright herb make a refreshing eye compress, said to relieve puffiness.

Nose: To relieve the nasal congestion of colds, pour boiling water over basil leaves and inhale the steam.

chapter 8.

A Brief History
of Herbs

ERBS HAVE BEEN part of human life since even
before *Homo sapiens*. At least six medicinal
herbs were found in a Neanderthal burial site
some 60,000 years old, evidence that our earliest ances-
tors had already acquired sophisticated knowledge of
the uses of plants.

By the time of the Sumerians, around 2500 B.C.,
herbal knowledge was beginning to be recorded on
tablets. The Egyptian Ebers papyrus—a 65-foot-long
roll written around 1550 B.C. and discovered in 1874
by a German Egyptologist—describes surgical proce-
dures, internal medicine, and many herbal remedies,
including the use of hemp for eye problems. Among
the 800 medicinal herbs in the Ebers papyrus are anise,
cassia, cardamom, thyme, and garlic. The Egyptians
were particularly fond of garlic, believing that it

strengthened the body and prevented disease.

In addition, virtually all the cultures of the ancient world certainly used herbs to create perfumes, dyes, cosmetics, and culinary flavorings.

The First Herbal

A written compilation of herbal knowledge, organized like an encyclopedia, is called an herbal. Herbals reveal a great deal about how people used herbs and about how herbs fit into their world view. Often written for a lay audience, herbals reflected folk beliefs as well as the scientific dogma of their day.

The first great herbal was China's *Pen Ts'ao Ching*, or *The Classic Herbal*, written around 2700 B.C. by the emperor Shen Nong, "the divine cultivator"—the same emperor credited with the discovery of the tea leaf, *Camellia sinensis*. According to legend, Shen Nong lived for a thousand years, aided in no small part by his transparent abdomen, which allowed him to observe the workings of his digestive system. As he tasted herbs and noted their effects, he learned which ones were beneficial and which were harmful—or even fatal. Eventually, he died permanently, leaving behind an important record of his vast store of knowledge.

The *Pen Ts'ao Ching* lists more than 300 herbal remedies made from a wide variety of plants, including ephedra or ma huang (one of the world's oldest cultivated plants, grown in China for more than 5,000 years), rhubarb, and opium poppy. The book also established a theory of Chinese medicine, based on five interrelated elements: wood, fire, earth, metal, and water. Good health, wrote Shen Nong, depends on the elements being in harmony, with a balance between yin and yang, the two complementary forces of energy representing dark and light, cold and heat, inertia and energy. The human body is seen as a microcosm of nature, and doctors are more akin to gardeners—pruning, fertilizing, and planting—than like the Western concept of medical mechanics.

The animating force of Chinese medicine is called Qi (pronounced "chee"), sometimes translated as "energy field." The flow of Qi along channels, or meridians, in the body, can be regulated by diet, exercise, acupuncture (stimulation with fine needles), and, of course, herbal medicine.

Many of the herbal remedies first described in the *Pen Ts'ao Ching* are still commonly used in Chinese medicine, some 4,700 years after it was written. Chinese herbs are prescribed as pills, powders, or decoctions—broths made in the patient's home from dried herbs.

The Ayurvedic Texts

Herbal medicine in India developed almost simultaneously with Chinese medicine. According to legend, the Hindu gods instructed the first human physicians in Ayurveda, "the science of life." These lessons were compiled in ancient texts called Vedas, the most ancient of which dates to 2500 B.C. One of the texts, the *Rig Veda*,

---

HEALING POWER EVERYWHERE

An Ayurvedic legend illustrates the central importance of herbs in Indian medicine. A disciple of Punarvasu Atreya, founder of India's first medical school, studied for seven years with the master. At the end of his apprenticeship, he asked Atreya when his training would be complete. "Go out into the countryside," said Atreya, "and bring back all the plants that have no medical use." The student set out on his quest, but returned empty handed after several days. "I could not find a single plant without healing power," he said sadly. Satisfied, Atreya responded: "Go! You are now ready to be a physician."

---

contains formulas for medicines combining 67 herbs, including ginger, cinnamon, senna, serpentwood (the source of a modern anti-asthmatic medicine reserpine), and garlic (with which ancient Ayurvedic healers claimed to have cured leprosy).

Like Chinese medicine, Ayurvedic medicine incorporated the concept of the human body as a microcosm of the cosmos, and was based on five elements: earth, water, fire, air, and ether (the nothingness that fills space). *Agni*, the digestive fire, converts the five elements into three body types, or humors: *vata* (wind), *pitta* (fire), and *kapha* (phlegm). Meditation, physical exercise, foods, and herbs are believed to be able to correct imbalances—for example, a person with an excess of phlegm would be treated with warm, light, dry foods such as hot spices and stimulating herbs.

Ayurvedic medicine has enjoyed a modest revival in

the West since the 1990s, thanks largely to the efforts of writers such as Deepak Chopra, M.D.

The Greek Contributions

The ancient Greeks assimilated herbal traditions from the realms they traded with or conquered, including Assyria, Persia, and Egypt. Aesculapias, who lived around 1250 B.C., is immortalized by the image associated with him, a staff with a snake entwined around it—the symbol used in the modern medical caduceus. The great Greek healer Hippocrates (460-377 B.C.), after whom the doctor's Hippocratic Oath is named, classified foods and herbs into four categories—cold, damp, dry, and hot—corresponding to the elements water, earth, air, and fire.

The ancient Greeks also left behind two great herbals, both written by Theophrastus of Eresus (circa 372-286 B.C.), a disciple of Aristotle. *Inquiry into Plants* and *Growth of Plants* described about 500 medicinal herbs.

The best-known Greek herbal was written in the first century A.D. by Dioscorides, a physician to the Roman army. *De Materia Medica*, as the herbal was called, was influenced by Egyptian traditions but represented a step backward. It discussed about 500 plants, but so vaguely and briefly that it is hard today to know exactly which ones were being described. Nevertheless, *De Materia Medica* became the foundation of herbal medicine for

127

the next 1,500 years. Well into the sixteenth century, it was still widely quoted and relied on.

The Roman Tradition

It is to the Romans that we owe our "modern" view of medicine as a mechanistic endeavor. Although the Romans absorbed Greek theories, they tended to view the body as a machine to be repaired. The outstanding exception to this view was Galen (131-199 A.D.), who was court physician to Emperor Marcus Aurelius. Galen revived Hippocrates' ideas and worked them into his own theories of the "humors"—bodily fluids corresponding to the four elements and their respective temperaments. Galen's views were hugely influential on European and Arab medicine for many centuries. The Canon of Medicine, written by the great eleventh-century Islamic doctor Avicenna, carried forward Galen's theories and documented the medicinal properties of many herbs; it was a textbook in European universities until the seventeenth century.

Into the Dark

With the fall of Rome in the fifth century A.D., Europe plunged into the Dark Ages. Scientific inquiry was actively discouraged, and non-Christian learning—including the wisdom of the Greeks, Romans, and Arabs—was suspect. Herbalism survived in Catholic monasteries where nuns and monks, usually the only literate members of the population, copied ancient texts and grew "physic gardens" containing plants that could be used in teas and remedies. Some of them experimented with Arabic elixirs, which resulted in the invention of still-famous herb-based liqueurs such as Chartreuse (named for Chartres, home of the great cathedral) and Benedictine (named for the order of monks that created it).

A few written herbals survive from the Dark Ages. The oldest, the Anglo-Saxon *Leech Book of the Bald,* dates from the first half of the tenth century. It describes many popular English herbs such as mugwort, vervain, and wood betony—used more as religious amulets than as remedies.

Folk herbalists, meanwhile, did what folk herbalists had always done: treat disease with plants as best they could. Illiteracy was widespread, so the oral tradition prevailed, but occasionally a sympathetic cleric would be moved to write down some local practices, usually without comment or criticism. Walahfrid Strabo, a

monk who lived in what is now Switzerland during the ninth century A.D., wrote such a collection in verse form. Of sage he wrote, "It holds the place of honor, is of good scent, and virtues for many ills"— some of which, he claimed, included palsy, indigestion, and toothache. Strabo also passed along an "antidote" to aconite, an extremely

Sage

Aconite

poisonous plant: "a dose of wholesome horehound." We know horehound today as a soothing ingredient in throat lozenges—and most assuredly no antidote to poison.

Hildegard of Bingen

A German Benedictine abbess and mystic, Hildegard of Bingen (1098-1179), claimed to be inspired by divine visions to compile her herbal formulas into a book, *Physica.* It is among the very few collections of the "old wives' tales" told by "wise women" who served as the doctors of the day. In it, Hildegard describes some 230 plants, including aloe, oats, and even St. John's Wort, a popular twenty-first-century remedy for depression.

Hildegard was "rediscovered" in the 1990s, and an English-language edition of her book, retitled *Hildegard's Healing Plants*, was published in 2001.

By 1300, similar "wise women"—a literal meaning of "witch"—were being persecuted and burned at the stake throughout Europe. As practitioners of herbal medicine, they were regarded by the Roman Catholic Church as confederates of the Devil. Healing preparations were condemned as poisons and aphrodisiacs.

One ray of light was the medical school in Salerno, Italy, which was founded on Hippocratic principles in the eleventh century and which brought together scholars from the Greek, Roman, Saracen, and Arabic cultures. The school's textbook was used throughout Western Europe for several centuries.

The Doctrine of Signatures

Herbal medicine flowered again in the European Renaissance, where it became known as "official" medicine. Hundreds of herbals were published; some actually contained useful information. Most mixed religion, superstition, astrology, and metaphysical doctrines with a bit of botanical lore.

Leading the movement to return to simpler medicine was Paracelsus, born near Zurich in 1493. Paracelsus espoused a dogma known as the Doctrine of Signature, which argued that the Creator had marked each plant with a "sign" of its benefits to man. The plant's outward appearance, therefore, was an indication of its use.

Because walnuts resembled the brain, for example, they were thought to stimulate mental activity. Yellow plants such as marigold and saffron were certainly meant to treat jaundice, which makes the skin yellow. And plants like mandrake, which looked like the human form, were believed to be God's gift to the entire body.

Despite its apparent absurdity to modern sensibilities, the Doctrine of Signatures was occasionally effective. And Paracelsus' teachings were on the whole less harmful than the powerful purgatives and emetics in vogue during his day.

Old World Meets New

From the eleventh century on, travel and exploration greatly expanded European knowledge about herbs and medicine, forever changing the world's food supply and health practices.

The Crusades of the eleventh through thirteenth centuries did more than introduce a new kind of religious war: They also brought back to Europe the comparatively sophisticated medical practices of the Middle East. In the Arab and Persian worlds, there had been no Dark Ages. Greek and Roman medicine had been preserved, studied, and further developed. In addition, the Near Eastern countries had their own indigenous herbs, which held great promise to Europeans.

Even more dramatic were the European voyages of exploration to the Americas. Along with gold and silver, the voyagers brought back a wealth of new food plants as well as those with medicinal benefits, such as cinchona, the Peruvian bark that is the source of the modern malaria drug quinine. The Europeans exported their herbs as well. Traveling eastward, sixteenth-century Dutch explorers brought sage to the Chinese, who became so fond of sage tea that they were willing to trade three pounds of their own *Camellia sinensis* tea for one pound of dried sage.

Sage tea was also a popular beverage among eighteenth-century American patriots who boycotted English tea imports. It was recommended by American doctors as late as the 1920s as a gargle for sore throats.

In 1652, Puritan herbalist and astrology buff Nicholas Culpeper wrote one of the most influential (and unreliable) herbals ever published in English, the *Complete Herbal and English Physician*. The first translation of Latin medical knowledge into English, it also touted the folk remedies of English country people. It has never since been out of print.

> *"The root boiled with liquorice, raisons, and aniseed is good for those troubled with cough. Also, it is of special value against the plague, the decoction thereof being drunk and the root smelled. The green herb being bruised and applied to the head taketh away pain and pricking thereof."*
>
> —Nicholas Culpeper on valerian, 1649

Herbs in the Americas

Although the indigenous people of North and South America did not leave written documents, by the time of the European conquests they had developed highly sophisticated herbal skills. Spanish observers in the sixteenth century noted that the Nahua of Mexico had a well-developed medical system. Cotton Mather, the Puritan minister and doctor, wrote admiringly in the late seventeenth century that North American Indian healers produced "many cures that are truly stupendous."

Among the herbs the Native Americans introduced to Europeans are some plants still used medicinally in

one form or another: black cohosh for menstrual pain and difficult childbirth, echinacea for colds and infections, slippery elm for sore throats. The Cherokee used goldenseal to treat arrow wounds; the Aztec used wild yams in poultices for boils; the Shoshone made a tea from lobelia leaves to induce vomiting.

These remedies, along with the Native North American healing tradition of sweathouses, were adapted by a New Hampshire-born medical man, Samuel Thomson, into an herb-based practice called Physiomedicalism that attracted as many as three

Lobelia

134

million adherents by the 1830s. Physiomedical healers used astringent and stimulant herbs to strengthen the body's "vital force" and keep body systems in balance— a concept very close to ancient Chinese and Indian doctrines.

Herbs in Modern Times

The premier English-language herbalist of the twentieth century was Mrs. Maud Grieve, whose two-volume *Modern Herbal* (1931) included detailed descriptions of more than 800 plants, from poisonous aconite to beneficial yerba santa. *A Modern Herbal* is still in print, and portions of it are viewable online (see Resources for Further Enjoyment).

When walked on, its strong, fragrant scent will often reveal its presence before it is seen. For this reason it was employed as one of the aromatic strewing herbs in the Middle Ages, and used often to be purposely planted in green walks in gardens. Indeed walking over the plant seems specially beneficial to it.

"Like a chamomile bed—
The more it is trodden
The more it will spread."

—Mrs. Maud Grieve on chamomile

The herbal tradition continues in many countries of the world to this day. In the less-developed countries, herbs are prescribed by traditional healers much as they have been for centuries. Throughout Asia, herbs are still the basis of traditional Chinese medicine, which combines as many as ten herbs into each formula. In the West, "alternative" medicine relies on herbal remedies, too, although generally preferring single-herb extracts such as ginkgo and ginseng.

Herbal infusions are popular throughout Europe; doctors often prescribe herbal extracts and homeopathic remedies that are sold in pharmacies (or "chemists' shops") alongside the products of pharmaceutical companies. Germany probably leads the world in scientific research into herbal medicine and in the efficient production of herbs as remedies.

Herbs on the Tongue

Meanings of some words commonly seen in herbals

Angelica: Once believed to have "angelic," or heavenly, powers. It is one of very few herbs nearly always referred to by its Latin, rather than common, name.

Chamomile: From the Greek words meaning "ground apple," a reference to the herb's fragrance and flavor.

Digitalis: The Latin name for foxglove means "of the finger," because the plant's flowers are finger-shaped.

Hyssop: This common name comes to us via Latin and Greek from the Hebrew *esob*, "holy herb," which is mentioned in the Old Testament. However, the Biblical plant was most likely some other herb—perhaps a species of marjoram.

Lavender: From the Latin *lavare*, to wash. Lavender was (and is) used for bathing, washing linens, and household cleaning.

Lady's Mantle: Plants with "lady" or "mother" in their names were frequently used in folk medicine to treat gynecological conditions such as heavy menstruation or difficult pregnancy.

Officinalis: As the second half of a Latin named (e.g., *Salvia officinalis*), this word indicates that the herb was once an "official" medicine.

Tussilago: From the Latin *tussis*, "cough." This herb, commonly called coltsfoot or coughwort, was once widely prescribed to coughing and wheezing patients.

Valerian: May come from the Latin *valere*, meaning "to be strong or healthy." Or it may be named in honor of Valerius, an early herbalist.

Wort: The Anglo-Saxon word for "plant," part of such common herb names as St. John's Wort, mugwort, soapwort, and milkwort.

chapter 9.

HERBS AND HEALTH

T RADITIONAL HERBAL medicine has a very long history. Archaeological evidence reveals that some 6,000 years ago, people in Mesopotamia (now Iraq) were using yarrow, marshmallow, and other healing herbs. Over the years, many valuable medicines have been extracted from plant sources—the heart medicine digitalis from foxglove, the malaria remedy quinine from cinchona, and the painkiller aspirin from willow bark are among the most ubiquitous.

Before scientific testing clarified matters, some herbs acquired reputations for being virtually omnipotent. Chamomile, for instance, was used to treat dozens of unrelated conditions, including fever, digestive problems, kidney stones, delayed menstruation, malaria, and typhus. Occasionally, the herbs must have indeed performed as advertised. Or perhaps the boiled water in

Foxglove

which they were infused was simply safer than untreated water from the local well or creek.

Until the early 1800s, most medicines were made from whole plants infused in water or alcohol or chewed raw. Doses were difficult to standardize, and effects varied wildly. That changed dramatically in 1803, when a German pharmacist isolated morphine from opium, the milky juice of the opium poppy. Morphine is the medicinally potent part of the plant—its "active principle." Throughout the nineteenth century, scientists searched for other active principles. By 1870 they had isolated caffeine from coffee, quinine from cinchona, cocaine from coca, and many other drugs from their plant sources.

The discovery of active principles led to standardized drug dosages, but it also had a drawback. Plants often contain more than one active principle, and many inactive substances; they work synergistically in the whole plant, one effect moderating another. When compounds are isolated, their effects are often much stronger and more dangerous than when the whole plant is infused in an herbal tea.

140

Whole herbs in the diet—for example, in herbal "tea"—have several benefits to health:

- ❦ They provide small, safe doses of plant pharmaceuticals (sometimes called "nutriceuticals").
- ❦ In combination, they produce synergistic effects that can be more beneficial than single herbs alone.
- ❦ Whole plants contain natural checks and balances that prevent unwelcome side effects.

Health Properties of Herbs

Here are some of the most common terms you may find associated with descriptions of herbs:

Adaptogens: Herbs believed to strengthen and enhance the immune system while helping the body cope with stress. Also known as "tonics." *Eleuthero (Siberian) ginseng, Panax ginseng, astragalus, echinacea, schizandra, licorice.*

Antibacterials: Herbs that fight infection. *Garlic, goldenseal, echinacea.*

Antidiarrheals: Plants that may relieve diarrhea. *Blackberry, carob, peppermint, wild strawberry.*

Antioxidants: Herbs that prevent cell breakdown or promote cell recovery. *Rooibos, yerba maté.*

Digestion enhancers: Teas that relax the intestines, promote the elimination of intestinal gas, or stimulate the digestive process. *Bergamot mint, peppermint,* *spearmint, rooibos, ginger, lemon thyme, anise seeds, anise hyssop.*

Nervines: Herbs that can stimulate or relax the nervous system. *Hops, kava, chamomile, lemon balm.*

Recovery teas: Teas that help soothe the symptoms of colds and flus. *White sage, wintergreen, ephedra.*

Sedatives: Teas that promote relaxation and sleep without interfering with dreams or producing narcotic hangovers. *Valerian, linden flowers, passionflower, hops, skullcap, lavender.*

Stimulants: Substances that increase the physiological functions of the body. *Yerba maté, ginger, cinnamon, cassia, cayenne pepper, cardamom, allspice, star anise.*

Some Healthful Herbs Used in Tea

Astragalus

Used in Chinese medicine for 2,000 years, astragalus is considered a "tonic" or "adaptogen" herb: It enhances the immune system and helps the body fight stress and infections. In many parts of Asia, it is an "official" medicine prescribed for colds and flu, shortness of breath, and general weakness and fatigue. Human and animal studies performed from the late 1970s on, mostly in China and Japan, found that astragalus appears to stimulate the secretion of interferon, a protein that interferes with virus growth. There have also been promising results in studies that tested astragalus's anticancer properties. Astragalus is considered a very safe herb with no known side effects. It's often combined with other herbs such as ginseng to create healthful teas.

Echinacea

Native Americans in the Great Plains area were well acquainted with the benefits of echinacea: They used it to treat coughs, colds, sore throats, and infections. The Dakota even used echinacea to treat their horses. Enterprising American pharmacists in the nineteenth and early twentieth centuries used echinacea in "patent medicines" touted as cure-alls. The advent of antibiotics caused echinacea to be all but forgotten, but today it is enjoying a spectacular resurgence in popularity along with scientific interest. Several German studies published in the 1990s found echinacea to be more effective than placebos against colds and upper respiratory tract infections. (However, an American study published in 1998 found no significant difference between echinacea and placebos in treating colds.) Echinacea has no single active principle, but appears to work synergistically to stimulate the nonspecific activity of the immune system. It also has anti-inflammatory properties when applied externally. It has no known side effects, and is considered a very safe herb. Unlike many roots, it has a rather pleasant flavor that lends itself well to infusions.

Eleuthero ("Siberian") Ginseng

Neither Siberian nor a true ginseng, eleuthero has been widely used in traditional Chinese and modern Russian medicine. ("Eleuthero" is a Greek word meaning "freedom.") The root of this plant (which grows in eastern Russia and northern China, but not in Siberia) contains substances that enhance physical and mental performance. For that reason, it's popular in Russia as an ingredient in sports drinks, and is used by people in stressful occupations to improve their stamina. Clinical and laboratory studies, performed mostly in Russia, suggest that eleuthero stimulates the body's immune function (although the way in which it does so is still unclear). It has antioxidant properties and can have beneficial effects on blood pressure. It is a very safe plant, with virtually no side effects and no known toxicity level.

Garlic

The "stinking rose," *Allium sativum*, has a long history as both a food and a medicine. The builders of the Egyptian pyramids were given garlic rations to keep their strength up; the Greek physician Hippocrates prescribed it for infections, pneumonia, and cancer. In the Middle Ages, French priests used garlic to protect against bubonic plague. Now modern science is confirming garlic's historical reputation. Garlic has been extensively researched: As of 1997, there were nearly

2,000 published studies of garlic's chemical or pharmacological properties (including some 200 studies on humans). Garlic has been shown to fight bacteria, lower blood cholesterol, improve circulation in the extremities, and protect against irregular heartbeat. Several studies have also pointed to garlic's protective effect against certain kinds of cancer, especially those of the gastrointestinal tract. Even when consumed in large quantities, garlic is exceptionally safe; its most notorious side effect is "garlic breath."

Ginger

Centuries ago, Chinese sailors chewed ginger to prevent seasickness. Now modern research confirms that those old salts knew their roots. Ginger contains enzymes that aid in digestion and help dispel intestinal gas. Although it doesn't work for everyone, many travelers find ginger to be a safe and effective remedy for motion sickness—one that doesn't cause drowsiness the way prescription and over-the-counter remedies can. Ginger was also shown to be more effective than a placebo in preventing morning sickness during pregnancy, and it can also help relieve the nausea associated with anesthesia. It has a warming effect that can be helpful in warding off cold and flu viruses. Ginger is added to many herbal blends to contribute a spicy, bracing note.

Ginseng

Ginseng's Latin name, *panax*, means "panacea" or cure-all, and the root's reputation amply justifies the appellation. Over the centuries, *Panax ginseng* has been prescribed as a cure for colds, coughs, depression, impotence, menstrual problems, arthritis, malaria, memory loss, diabetes, high blood cholesterol, and cancer. It's been

Ginseng

used in Asian medicine for more than 5,000 years, mostly as a general strengthening tonic, and is an often-prescribed "official" drug in Germany, Austria, Switzerland, and France. The Chinese name for ginseng, *ren shen*, means "man root"—the plant does somewhat resemble a human form, and some observers believed that if it looked like a man, it must be beneficial for the ills of man. The legendary Chinese emperor Shen Nong asserted that "continuous use [of ginseng] leads to longevity," and many claims have been made for ginseng's value as an aphrodisiac and a whole-body tonic. There have been many laboratory and clinical studies of ginseng's effects, but the research has been of varying quality. Some of the better studies have found that ginseng improves energy and alertness in elderly people, athletes, and manual workers. In addition, ginseng contains compounds called ginsenosides—antioxidants that can prevent conditions that lead to heart disease. It's believed that ginseng strengthens the body's response to stress by moderating hormonal reactions, and

146

that it does so on an individual, idiosyncratic basis: For example, depending on the body's need, it can enhance either energy or sleep.

Valerian

With sleep disorders reportedly on the rise, it's a good time to become reacquainted with "nature's tranquilizer." Valerian has a calming, mildly sedative effect that has been shown in randomized, double-blind clinical studies to produce significantly better sleep quality and lower levels of anxiety. Just how valerian works, though, is still unclear. A 1989 study indicated that it binds to benzodiazepine receptors in the brain in much the same way as prescription tranquilizers such as Valium, although in a milder manner. Interestingly, for much of its history valerian was recommended for nearly every-thing *except* insomnia. The ancient Greeks and Romans used it to treat digestive disorders, menstrual cramps, nausea, and epilepsy, among other disorders. In the nineteenth century, it was prescribed for hysteria and "the vapors." Today, it's often combined with other sleep-inducing herbs such as hops, passionflower, or skullcap—as well as with sweet or flowery plants that mask valerian's bitterness.

Rooibos

Sometimes called the national drink of South Africa, rooibos (or "red tea") is one of the most versatile and healthful of herbs. Since the end of the Apartheid-era sanctions in 1993, it has become better known—and more widely enjoyed—outside its native habitat. Rooibos is one of the few herbs that is as tasty as it is beneficial: It is low in astringency-producing tannins and bitterness, and has a "flavor profile" very similar to that of black tea. Like black tea, rooibos is oxidized ("fermented") or semi-fermented; unlike black tea, it has no caffeine. Like green tea, it is rich in healthy antioxidants—in particular super oxide dismutase, an enzyme that functions as a prime scavenger of free radicals and prevents fats from changing into harmful lipid peroxide—and polyphenols. Rooibos also contains iron, potassium, calcium, copper, zinc, manganese, and fluoride. Because it has no caffeine and very little tannin, rooibos won't inhibit the absorption of iron, the mineral essential to healthy energy levels that is deficient in many women. Its antispasmodic properties may help relieve stomach and digestive problems such as nausea, vomiting, heartburn, and stomach ulcers; in South Africa, it's mixed with milk and given to colicky babies. It's also recommended for a wide variety of ailments from nervous tension and hay fever to insomnia. No independent laboratory or clinical studies have yet been performed on rooibos in the United States. Japanese studies have shown rooibos to have antiviral properties that come from its oligosaccharides (simple sugars)—which also make rooibos naturally mildly sweet.

Yerba Maté

First brewed by the Guaraní Indians and now the national drink of Argentina, yerba maté is a drink of sociability and good health. The ground-up leaves of this relative of the holly bush are rich in vitamins and minerals, including vitamins A, C, and B, magnesium, and potassium. Its antioxidant properties come from the polyphenols in its leaves, which produce health benefits similar to those of green tea. Maté is first and foremost a stimulant: It contains all three xanthine stimulants—caffeine, theophylline, and theobromine—that are found in varying amounts in coffee, tea, and chocolate. Maté's caffeine level is similar to that of a cup of green tea. Because of this caffeine, maté temporarily increases alertness and dilates the bronchial tubes, which can produce temporary relief from asthmatic symptoms. People who are sensitive to caffeine should avoid maté. People who desire a milder stimulant than coffee will find that maté produces fewer jitters and less nervous tension. Maté fans believe it makes them calmer!

About Homeopathy

The medical practice of homeopathy uses tiny—even microscopic—doses of plant extracts to cure disease symptoms that the same plants would cause in larger doses. It was first formulated in 1810 by a devoutly religious German physician, Samuel Hahnemann, who theorized the Law of Similars—"like cures like." One of his first cures involved quinine, extracted from the Peruvian cinchona tree: It causes fevers in healthy people and relieves them in patients with malaria. Quinine is still used to treat malaria today. Homeopathy was a dramatic departure from the common medical practices of Hahnemann's time, which involved huge doses of poisons such as mercury as well as bloodletting and radical surgery. It is still practiced today, sometimes with remarkable success; in many countries, including England, France, Greece, India, and Sri Lanka, it is on equal footing with more conventional medical practices.

The Dietary Supplement Health and Education Act

The most significant landmark in the recent history of the U.S. herb industry was the Dietary Supplement Health and Education Act (DSHEA). Passed unanimously by Congress in 1994, DSHEA defines dietary supplements and allows them to bear health benefit claims that describe the supplements' effect on the structure or function of the body. These claims must be supported by scientific evidence and accompanied by a medical disclaimer, but do not need prior government approval.

Since the passage of DSHEA, major drug companies have found a financial incentive in developing and marketing "alternative" herbal remedies, and herbal products have multiplied on U.S. drugstore and supermarket shelves. Many people are hopeful that DSHEA will clear the way for a new era of scientific research into traditional remedies.

A Cautionary Note

Herbs are natural substances, but that does not mean all herbs are equally safe for all people. Reactions may range from sneezing and sniffling to intestinal cramps, vomiting, and even death from some highly toxic plants such as foxglove (digitalis). Never experiment with wild-picked herbs; when you are trying a new herbal infusion, sample a little bit at a time until you are sure it agrees with you. If you are pregnant or nursing, consult your physician before taking herbal supplements.

Exercise particular caution with the following herbs:

Comfrey (*Symphytum officinale*) contains liver toxins and should not be taken internally.

Ephedra (in Chinese medicine, *ma huang*) was the subject of considerable controversy in the 1990s, when it was widely used in over-the-counter weight-loss products and was abused as a recreational drug. Ephedra can be a useful allergy remedy, but should not be combined with caffeine or other stimulants.

Sassafras, native to North America, is not allowed in food products in the United States. The major constituent of its volatile oil is thought to be harmful to the liver.

Licorice contains glycyrrhizin, a substance similar to the hormone cortisol. People who have hypertension (high blood pressure), diabetes, severe kidney insufficiency, or cirrhosis of the liver should not use whole licorice root or isolated gylcyrrhizin. It's also best to avoid it during pregnancy.

Senna, a powerful stimulant laxative, is used in some "natural" diet and detoxification products. Its effects vary widely, and its potential for abuse makes it controversial and even risky. Other stimulant laxatives to avoid are cascara sagrada, aloe latex, and rhubarb root.

chapter 10.

A GUIDE TO HERBS
USED IN TEA

I N HER 1931 CLASSIC, *A Modern Herbal*, Mrs. Maud Grieve gave detailed descriptions of more than 800 herbs. Our own list is more selective, being limited to those plants used to create tasty or healthful herbal infusions. We've classified them according

Spearmint

to the parts most frequently used for tea (for example, Rosehips and Rose Petals are listed separately). Within each category, the plants are listed alphabetically.

Berry Leaves

Blackberry (*Rubus fruticosus, R. villosus*): The leaves taste nothing like the fruit; their flavor is neutral, with an astringent note that comes from their tannin content. It must be blended with other herbs and spices to be palatable. Frequently used as a base for herbal teas because it has a similar color and flavor as black tea. Both species (European and North American) used for many centuries to cure a number of disorders, including diarrhea, dysentery, mouth sores, and gum inflammation.

Chinese Sweet Blackberry (*Rubus suavissimus*): This leaf is the only blackberry species that combines sweetness and astringency; if leaves are harvested too early, the sweetness fails to develop fully. Native to the mountains around Guilin, in central China. Because the Japanese are very interested in the plant and are actively researching it, supplies are scarce. It produces an infusion with a good body.

Raspberry (*Rubus idaeus*): Often found in pregnancy teas because of its traditional reputation for preventing

miscarriage and easing childbirth. Twentieth-century British researchers confirmed that a constituent of the leaf, fragarine, can both stimulate and relax uterine tissue. The astringent, rather unpleasant leaves must be combined with other herbs to be palatable.

Strawberry (*Fragaria vesca, F. americana*): Not as astringent as other berry leaves yet still "puckery" enough to substitute for black tea in blends. Originally wildcrafted in Eastern Europe; now

154

harvested from commercially grown fields as a secondary product to the fruit.

Fermented Herbs

Rooibos (*Aspalathus linearis*) ROY-boss: Dutch for "red bush," this shrub with needle-like leaves grows only in the Cedarberg area near Cape Town, South Africa. For at least a century, locals there have made an aromatic tea by harvesting the wild plants, bruising them with hammers, and allowing them to oxidize, or ferment, before drying them in the sun. In 1904, a Russian immigrant with family connections in the tea industry began marketing rooibos (or rooibosch, as it's sometimes spelled); by the middle of the twentieth century, research into rooibos's health benefits was yielding promising results. Rooibos is known to have antioxidant properties, with no caffeine and very little tannin; it produces a deep-red cup with a round, "full" taste—comparable in body and depth to black tea—without bitterness, sweetness, or astringency. It combines well with milk, and is often used to lend body and color to herb tea blends. South African studies have found it to boost the immune system and relieve insomnia, stomach cramps, and colic.

Flowers

Chamomile (*Matricaria chamomilla* or *Anthemis nobilis*): Fragrance is sweet and apple-like (the ancient

155

Botswana Blossom Smoothie

Rooibos lends color and health to this refreshing blender drink.

> *1 cup of iced Botswana Blossom rooibos tea*
> *1/2 banana*
> *5 oz. Pineapple*
> *1/4 cup sweetened coconut milk*
> *2 cups ice*

Pour all ingredients into blender. Blend and serve.

Greeks called it "ground apple"; in Spanish it is "manzanilla," or "little apple"); taste is floral with a bitter afternote. One of the most popular tea herbs in the world; drunk as a single herb tea and also blended with lemon-flavored herbs, linden flowers, and other flowers. The two plants known as chamomile come from unrelated species, yet have similar daisy-like flowers and long histories in folk medicine. Used to treat malaria in ancient Egypt and indigestion in medieval Germany; infusion is often recommended for irritable bowel syndrome, anxiety, and insomnia. *Anthemis*, also known as Roman chamomile, is the species commonly used in tea; *Matricaria*

Chamomile flower

156

chamomile, also known as German chamomile, is considered inferior.

Hibiscus (*Hibiscus sabdariffa*): Tangy and refreshing; contains citric and other acids and large quantities of vitamin C, calcium, niacin, riboflavin, and iron. It's usually found in blends with fruits and spices; popular both hot and iced. Turns tea a bright-red color. Not to be confused with ornamental hibiscus (*H. rosa-sinensis*), it's a bushy shrub sometimes grown for its jute-like fiber; the calyces (leaf-like enclosures of unopened flower buds) are the parts used in tea. Originally native from India to Malaysia; naturalized in Africa, the West Indies, Central America, Thailand, and China.

Lavender (*Lavandula officinalis*, *L. angustifolia*, and other species): Tastes the way it smells: sharp, perfumy, aromatic. It's too strong to be drunk without blending; in blends, it provides a distinct top spike of flavor and a refreshing quality. Only unfaded, deep-blue flowers should be used; they turn tea a purplish-blue color. May have originated in India, but quickly made its way to the Mediterranean; still an important commercial crop in the south of France. "Lavender" comes from Latin *lavare*, "to wash"; lavender was traditionally used for bathing and housecleaning. Dried lavender in a pillow is a folk remedy for insomnia. Lavender is also used widely in cooking and baking, and is said to have digestive benefits.

Lavender

Linden Blossoms (*Tilia cordata*): One of the few herbs that is more popular today than in ancient or medieval times. Linden blossoms have a deliciously sweet, flower-nectar flavor. Blossoms are picked by hand by harvesters standing on tall ladders to reach the tops of the trees; it takes many blossoms to yield a single pound. Because of high labor costs, linden blossoms are rare in commercial U.S. tea blends, but are very popular in Europe. Linden tea is reputed to soothe nervous complaints, lower blood pressure, and aid digestion.

Orange Blossoms (*Citrus aurantium*): Flowery orange-nectar flavor; very popular in herbal tea blends. Petals are collected as they fall to the ground after the flowers have been fertilized; quality varies. According to Mrs. Maud Grieve, author of *A Modern Herbal* (1931), an infusion of the flowers alone was traditionally drunk by Europeans as a mild nervous stimulant. Other sources claim it's a sedative.

Rose Petals (*Rosa spp.*): Mildly astringent; delicate floral nectar flavor. Originally cultivated by the cultures occupying the ancient Near East; spread to ancient Greece and Italy. Tea rose (*R. indica*) named for resemblance of its fragrance to black tea.

Fruits

Black Currant (*Ribes nigrum*): An aromatic berry native to Europe. The fruit is very high in vitamin C, and the dried leaves have a long history as a folk remedy for rheumatism and gout. Black currant is one of a handful of plants whose seeds are a rich source of gamma-linolenic acid (GLA), which is a building block for hormone-like compounds known as anti-inflammatory prostaglandins. Research done with GLA from another plant, evening primrose, has suggested benefits in cases of premenstrual syndrome, diabetic neuropathy, and breast pain.

Elderberries (*Sambucus nigra, S. edulus*): The elder tree has a long history in English folklore; its bark, leaves, and flowers are all used in various medicinal and cosmetic preparations (elderflower water is still used in some skin lotions). Fermented berries are used to make wine. Infusions made from the berries were traditionally used to treat constipation and rheumatism.

Hawthorn Berries (*Crataegus laevigata, C. oxycantha*): Frequently found in European herbal medications, hawthorn berries have the same antioxidants found in tea and grapes. Medicinally, hawthorn has been in widespread use only since the late 1800s—and hardly at all in the United States. It is considered a very safe cardiovascular tonic, with no known side effects, and is used to treat high blood pressure, nervous disorders, insomnia, and congestive heart failure.

Lemon Peel and Juice (*Citrus limonum*): Bright, tangy-tart flavor. Lemon juice in concentrate is a natural flavor enhancer for herbal teas. High in vitamin C; famous for its role in defeating "sailor's scourge," scurvy. Wild lemon trees probably originated in northern India; brought to Europe by Arab traders.

Orange Peel (*Citrus aurantium*): Stronger flavor than orange blossoms: rich, full, signifying presence of orange oil. Used for centuries to flavor food and tea; source of "orange" in most orange-spice tea combinations. First introduced to the West by the Arabs, it's now cultivated through the world's temperate zone, most notably Spain, Israel, Florida, and California.

Rosehips (*Rosa canina*): Tart, fruity flavor; turns infusion a reddish-brown. It's typically mixed with 20 percent to 30 percent hibiscus as the flavors and colors are complementary. Vitamin C content is higher than that of oranges, ounce for ounce; also high in vitamins A, B,  E, and K, as well as organic acids and pectins that make rosehips mildly laxative and diuretic. Rosehips are the fruit of the dog rose, a wild variety that is the original source of cultivated roses.

Lemon-Flavored Herbs

Lemon Balm (*Melissa officinalis*): Mellow, flowery, soothing lemon flavor. Popular in France in teas; known there as Thé de France. Blends well with chamomile. Main flavoring ingredient in Benedictine and Chartreuse liqueurs. Named by the Greeks for the bees (*Melissa*) that hover around it, but not to be confused with "bee balm." Considered a "universal remedy" in

folk medicine, good for gastrointestinal upset, liver and gallbladder problems, menstrual trouble, and colds. Also a mild sedative.

Lemon Grass (*Cymbopogon citratus*): Invigorating citronelle lemon note that hits high in the mouth. Popular culinary addition in Thailand and Vietnam; also found growing in Central America. It grows in clumps of tall grass and is closely related to citronella, whose oil is a popular insect repellent. In India and Sri Lanka, lemon grass is known as "fever tea," and is combined with other herbs to treat fever, diarrhea, and stomachaches. Used in Brazil and the Caribbean for nervous and digestive problems; traditionally used in Cuba to reduce blood pressure. In Chinese medicine, used to treat headaches, stomachaches, colds, and rheumatic pains. Contains five constituents that inhibit blood coagulation.

Lemon Myrtle (*Backhousia citriodora*): Lemon-flavored leaf from a rainforest tree native to Australia. The oil of lemon myrtle contains 90 percent citral, compared to only 3 percent for lemon oil, which makes lemon myrtle leaves even more intensely lemony than lemon itself. They also have a hint of lime flavor. Used for tea and as a seasoning in cooking.

Lemon Thyme (*Thymus serpullum, var. citriodorus*): Fragrant round thyme flavor with a lemon tone. Blends well with ginger and mints. A variety of wild thyme; thymol, its active constituent, has strong antiseptic properties and can be helpful with digestive and respiratory complaints. Morocco and Hungary produce lemon

161

thyme for the European market; grown organically in the Pacific Northwest of the U.S.

Lemon Verbena (*Aloysia triphylla*; also called *Lippia citriodora*): Deep, refreshing, perfumy lemon flavor. Re-

lated only in common name to verbena, or vervain (*Verbena officinalis*). Native to the Americas; brought to Europe by Spanish conquerors of Chile and Argentina. In South America, lemon verbena tea is given to asthmatics; also reputed to have digestive properties similar to the mints and lemon balm.

Mints

Bergamot Mint (*Mentha piperita, var. citrata*): Unique perfumy flavor compared both to lavender and to Bergamot oranges (the flavoring ingredient in Earl Grey tea). Sometimes called eau de Cologne mint or orange mint; said to have the same digestive properties attributed to the other members of the mint family.

Peppermint (*Mentha piperita*): Cool menthol flavor with pleasant sharpness; slightly astringent. Used alone or in blends, hot or iced. Apparently unknown in the ancient world, peppermint was first documented in 1696 by an English botanist, John Ray. It was listed in the 1721 *London Pharmacopeia* as a digestive aid and flavoring agent. Its essential oil, menthol, stimulates the flow of bile to the stomach and aids digestion.

Spearmint (*Mentha spicata*): Milder and sweeter than peppermint; more widely used in cooking. Commonly known as a toothpaste or chewing gum flavor. Thought to be the oldest of all mints; mentioned in the Bible and enjoyed by Romans and Arabs of the ancient world. Widely used as a digestive aid.

Other Aromatic Herbs

Anise Hyssop (*Agastache foeniculum, A. rugosa*): Light, sweet, anise-scented flavor; flowers and leaves are used in herb tea blends. Neither an anise nor a hyssop, the plant is a member of the mint family and a native of North America from Ontario to the Midwest of the United States; originally cultivated for its beautiful blue flowering spikes. Chippewa and Cheyenne Indians traditionally used anise hyssop as a food sweetener and to treat respiratory problems and chest pains. Related Chinese giant hyssop grows wild in China, Korea, Japan, and Taiwan; according to traditional Chinese medicine, it "opens the stomach" and is used as a carminative, to stop vomiting, for colds and flu, and for angina pains.

Rosemary (*Rosemarinus officinalis*): Fresh, strongly aromatic, wholly characteristic fragrance and flavor. Used in herbal tea blends. In Chinese medicine,

163

rosemary leaves are mixed with ginger to treat headaches, indigestion, insomnia, and malaria; a traditional European remedy for poor circulation is rosemary extracted into white wine. Name, meaning "dew of the sea," comes from its deep-blue flowers and preferred habitat along seacoasts.

Sage (*Salvia officinalis*): Intense camphor flavor. Enjoyable mixed with honey and lemon—a combination traditionally used to soothe sore throats. Documented use as early as 1600 B.C., in Crete. Found growing wild around the Mediterranean; widely naturalized. Name comes from Latin *salvare*, "to heal or save." Contains a strong antioxidant and antibacterial agent that was used to preserve meat (especially sausage). Has been used to treat a wide range of ailments, including mouth sores, headaches, hemorrhoids, depression, and palsy. Many folk traditions included a belief that sage would lengthen a person's life if taken regularly.

Thyme (*Thymus vulgaris, T. zygis*): Pungent and slightly bitter. Native to the western Mediterranean and naturalized widely. Was used medicinally in ancient Sumeria (in poultices) and Egypt (to embalm the dead). Romans used it to flavor cheese. Essential oil contains thymol, which is antibacterial and antifungal; frequently added to cough drops and gargles. Thyme infusion can clear upper-respiratory congestion and calm coughs.

White Sage (*Salvia apiana*): Common name of a low shrub native to the arid coastal hills and plains of California. Native Americans wrapped sage into bundles that were burned during sweat-lodge ceremonies. In tea, white sage adds a spike of pungent flavor that immediately makes its presence known. Sage tea is renowned for its ability to combat sore throats, coughs, and colds; sage oil has strong antibacterial and antifungal properties.

Wintergreen (*Gaultheria procumbens*): An evergreen shrub native to the eastern United States and Canada, wintergreen is best known as a minty-tasting flavoring for toothpaste and candy. Native Americans traditionally used the leaves as a soothing agent for fever and sore throats. Wintergreen's volatile oils contain methyl salicylate, the same pain-relieving compound found in aspirin.

Rainforest Herbs and Spices

Allspice (*Pimenta officinalis, P. dioica*): Combines the flavors of cloves, cinnamon, nutmeg, and pepper. Berries are used in cooking; leaves are used for tea—

they produce a full-bodied infusion with a flavor similar to that of the berries. Native to Central America, Mexico, and the West Indies. Berries, which resemble black peppercorns ("pimientas" in Spanish), were brought to Europe by the Spaniards in the sixteenth century.

165

Pau d'Arco (*Tabebuia impetiginosa* or *hepaphylla*) pow DARK-oh: Pleasant, full-bodied flavor; tea is dark red. Can be drunk by itself or blended. Inner bark or heartwood of the tree is used; careful harvesting techniques permit gathering inner bark without killing the tree. *Tabebuia* species grow in rainforests from Mexico to Argentina, and many Indian tribes claim various medicinal uses for it. Pau d'arco has powerful antibiotic and virus-killing properties, possibly related to its ability to increase oxygen circulation. It has been shown to be effective against candida and other disease organisms. In addition, studies performed at the University of Munich show that low dosages of pau d'arco have immunostimulating properties similar to those of echinacea.

Vanilla (*Vanilla planifolia*): Sweet, full, heady, complex flavor. Dried beans of an orchid, or their liquid extract, used to flavor herbal and black tea blends. The only member of the orchid family to be used for food; discovered by Mexican Indians before the Spanish conquest. Cultivated in many tropical parts of the world; vanilla from Mexico and Madagascar is considered the finest. Vanilla production is very labor-intensive: Flowers must be hand-pollinated and each bean handled some 400 times during the curing process. No medicinal claims.

Yerba Maté (*Ilex paraguariensis*) YER-ba ma-TAY: An acquired taste—infusion is bitter, astringent, and unpleasant at first, like black coffee. Native to Brazil, Paraguay, and Argentina, where it's made into a thick

166

paste and drunk, hot, from a hollowed-out gourd ("maté" in Spanish) through a tube ("bombilla") with a filter at one end to screen out the sediment. In Paraguay, it's also brewed into a cold beverage called *teréré*, which is drunk from a hollowed-out cow horn. The leaves are sold either green or roasted; the latter have a pleasant toasty flavor. Rich in vitamin C, polyphenols, and caffeine—a cup contains about as much caffeine as a cup of green tea. The Guaraní Indians of Paraguay used it as a stimulant and scurvy preventive in their all-meat diet. Today it's cultivated extensively in Argentina, where maté drinking is a social event that can last several hours.

Yerba Santa Acuyo (*Piper sanctum*): Unique spicy anise flavor. Large, heart-shaped leaves (twelve to sixteen inches across) used in tea and cooking. Related to pepper and many other food plants. Found growing by waterways in the middle altitudes of the rainforests in southern Mexico. A staple of Central American cuisine since before the Spanish invasion; popularly included there in tamales, salsas, fish and egg dishes, and digestive and bronchial teas.

Roasted Herbs and Roots

Barley (*Hordeum vulgare*): Adds a dark, grainy flavor and color to herb teas. Barley malt, made from dried germinated grain, is often used in tea for its high sugar content. Roasted barley is a popular substitute for coffee. Cultivated since Neolithic times; esteemed by ancient Egyptians and Greeks for nutritive qualities. Beer made from fermented barley was one of the earliest alcoholic beverages.

Carob Pods (*Ceratonia siliqua*): Sweet, round, roasted flavor without bitterness. Roasted, powdered pods are cut into small pieces to flavor herbal blends; good complements include cinnamon and the mints. Often substituted for chocolate because of comparable color and flavor. Tall evergreen tree native to southwestern Europe and western Asia. Derives name from "carat": Seeds were once used as a counterweight in measuring gold. Traditional diarrhea remedy.

Chicory Root (*Cichorium intybus*): Pleasantly bitter "roasted" flavor; adds dark color to tea. Often added to coffee, famously in Louisiana blends; reputed to mellow

 the caffeine effects. Perennial herb cultivated as far back as Egyptian times; common sight along North American highways. Cultivated much more extensively in Europe than in United States. Young greens are eaten in salads. Contains inulin, a soluble fiber good for digestion and elimination; drinking chicory daily can help increase beneficial microflora in the intestines and decrease toxic organisms such as candida. Belgian endive and radicchio (rocket) are varieties of Chichorium.

Sleep-inducing Herbs

Hops (*Humulus lupulus*): Bitter, unpleasant; must be blended with other ingredients to be palatable. Because of
bitterness, used in very small quantities
in commercial herb teas. Acts as a preservative and flavoring agent in beer; causes

familiar drowsiness after "one too many"; transforms
sweet ale into bitter beer. A perennial vine and member
of the hemp family, hops is native to Europe and North
America. One of the few crop plant species that bear
male and female flowers on different plants; only female
flowers are used in brewing and in medicine. In the
Middle Ages, hops were used as a gallbladder and liver
remedy. Contains humulon and lupulon, which have
antibiotic and sedative effects. European folk belief:
Sleeping on a pillow stuffed with crushed dried hops
will cure insomnia.

Kava (*Piper methysticum*): Bitter-tasting; pungent.
Also known as kava-kava, this root is native to the
South Pacific, where for centuries it has been prepared
in a thick brew and served on ritual occasions. ("Kava"
is derived from the Greek word for "intoxicating.")
Captain Cook and his botanists "discovered" the
plant—a member of the pepper family—on their first
South Pacific expedition in 1768. Kava has a calming,
slightly euphoric effect on the nervous system; at least

169

seven high-quality clinical studies have shown it to be of benefit in the treatment of anxiety, nervousness, and stress. Kava also appears to relax muscle tissue, and may help relieve mild pain.

Passion Flower (*Passiflora incarnata*): Mild, straw-like flavor, attributable to abundance of stem used along with leaf. Flowers and fruiting tops are soothing and can be mildly sedative in an infusion. Often combined with other calmative herbs such as lemon balm, valerian, and hops. Native to southern United States and Mexico; wildcrafted in southeastern United States; state flower of Tennessee. Discovered by a Spanish missionary in Mexico who saw symbolic elements of the Crucifixion in the flower's structure; named for the Passion of the Cross.

Skullcap (*Scutelleria lateriflora*): Green, alfalfa-like flavor. Often included in relaxing tea blends. Whole plant is harvested; cultivated plants are more pleasant-tasting than wildcrafted ones. Native to the southern part of the United States, where it was used by Native

Americans for rabies and menstrual problems before being adopted by European herbalists. Flavonoid glycosides in skullcap's volatile oil are responsible for its effects as a tranquilizer and sedative. A related species, *S. baicalensis*, is known as *huang qin* in China, where it's used to treat respiratory ailments.

Tilia (*Terstronemia spp.*): Deep, dark flavor completely unlike that of botanically unrelated *Tilia europea*,

the seed has matured. Used in tea and cooking. Originated in the Moluccas, five small islands in the southern Pacific, also known as the Spice Islands because of their botanical riches.

Ginger (*Zingiber officinale*): Invigorating, pungent flavor with a peppery "bite." Chopped or pow-  dered root used in cooking; chopped fresh root makes a fine tea—boil for five to ten minutes, strain, add honey and lemon. Native to Southeast Asia, where the Chinese discovered it and began employing it for medicine and as a spice. Ancient Greeks imported it from China; in the early sixteenth century, the Spanish began cultivating a superior-quality ginger in Jamaica. Today, the best ginger comes from the Caribbean. In Chinese medicine, it's used to treat colds and encourage sweating. East Africans use it to reduce headaches and kill internal parasites. Effective against motion sickness and pregnant women's morning sickness.

Mace and Nutmeg (*Myristica fragrans*): Aromatic, sweet; mace is subtler than nutmeg. Both are used to flavor food and tea. Derived from the same plant: Mace is the dried brittle yellow covering of the nutmeg  seed. Cultivated in tropical rainforests of the East and West Indies, Costa Rica, India, Sri Lanka, and Brazil. Used in China since the seventh century as a carminative

173

and digestive stimulant. In large enough amounts, it is a powerful hallucinogen.

Peppercorns (*Piper nigrum*): Hot, piquant. Traditionally used in Indian spice tea, or chai. Pepper berries are collected unripe and sundried to produce black pepper; or ripe and with hulls removed to produce less-piquant white pepper. Native to rainforests of India; mentioned in Sanskrit texts from fourth century B.C. Quest for pepper drove the spice trade and made many Arabs and Venetians rich. In early European history, peppercorns were used as currency.

Star Anise (*Illicum verum*): Sharp, spicy flavor, deeper than that of aromatic anise seeds. The Dutch began using it to flavor tea in seventeenth century, imitating the Chinese custom.  Fruit is star-shaped, with glossy brown seedpods contained in the points of the star. Originated in southern China and northern Vietnam. Star anise's essential oil is a flavor replacement for the more expensive aniseed oil in liqueurs such as anisette. Star anise is used in Chinese medicine as a carminative, stimulant, and diuretic.

Sweet Herbs

Anise (*Pimpinella anisum*): Sweet and aromatic. Famous flavoring agent of beverages from digestive teas to Turkish arrack, Greek ouzo, and French anisette. Member of the Umbelliferae family that also includes dill, fennel, caraway, angelica, and cumin; cultivated in the

Mediterranean region since the time of the Pharaohs. Its essential oil is identical to that of cheaper, stronger-flavored star anise, which has largely replaced aniseed oil commercially. All the Umbelliferaes are esteemed for their carminative (gas-dispelling) properties. Anise is used in cough medicines and lozenges; it relaxes the chest and relieves lung congestion.

Carob (*Ceratonia siliqua*): Pods abound in natural sugars yet are low in calories and fat, high in B vitamins and calcium. Also see section on roasted grains.

Chinese Sweet Blackberry: See berry leaves.

Licorice (*Glycyrrhiza glabra*): Sweet, somewhat "rooty." Often used in teas to mask the taste of bitter herbs, especially the tonic herbs, and to add its own characteristic flavor. Glycyrrhizin, one of its primary constituents, is 50 times sweeter than sucrose (sugar). Licorice appears in early Egyptian papyri; a bundle of licorice sticks was found in King Tut's tomb. Native Americans in the eastern United States used licorice tea as a cough remedy and laxative. Deglycyrrhizinated licorice is an effective remedy for duodenal ulcers, without the side effects of popular prescription remedies. Native to the Mediterranean and parts of Asia; grown commercially in Turkey, Greece, and Asia. Ninety percent of imported licorice is used by the tobacco industry to flavor cigarettes. Licorice candy contains no licorice at

175

all, but is flavored with similar-tasting anise oil. Non-deglycyrrhizinated licorice, if taken in sufficient quantities, can cause potentially dangerous water-retention and should be avoided by people with high blood pressure, diabetes, and kidney or liver illness.

Stevia (*Stevia rebaudiana*) STEE-vya: Intensely sweet; almost unpalatable at full strength. Excellent blended with bitter or bland herbs. Contains no calories yet is 300 times sweeter than cane sugar. Used for more than 400 years by the Guaraní Indians of Paraguay to sweeten food and teas. Contemporary Japanese scientists have done extensive research on stevia and use stevia extracts to flavor many foods and diet beverages. Unfortunately, stevia is available in the U.S. only as a dietary supplement because the Food and Drug Administration has blocked its use as a sweetener.

Tonic herbs

Astragalus (*Astragalus membranaceus*) uh-STRAG-uh-lus: Slightly sweet-tasting root known as *huang qi* ("yellow energy") in Chinese medicine. Usually used in combination with other botanicals such as ginseng. Astragalus has been prescribed in China for millennia as a treatment for colds and pulmonary ailments and to strengthen the immune system. A topical form of astragalus is used to treat chronic wounds.

Echinacea (*Echinacea angustifolia, E. purpurea*) eh-kin-AY-sha: Caramel root flavor, with hint of licorice.

176

Derived from the purple coneflower, a type
of aster native to North America east of
the Rocky Mountains. Native American
Plains Indians used echinacea as a tonic
and as a treatment for wounds and snakebite. Roots are
used alone in medicinal extracts; in teas, the roots are
usually blended with other botanicals for better flavor.
Since 1996, echinacea has been the best-selling herb in
the United States. There have been more than 350 scientific studies, mostly in Germany, of echinacea's medicinal effects; echinacea extract has been found to
shorten the duration of cold and flu symptoms and stimulate the nonspecific activity of the immune system.
Echinacea appears to be most effective when taken at
the first sign of an infection, rather than on a continuous, preventive basis.

Eleuthero Ginseng (*Eleutherococus senticosus*) eh-
LOO-ther-row: Pleasantly neutral bark flavor; produces
a light yellow tea. Dried, pulverized roots are used for
tea as well as for medicines. Commonly, if somewhat
misleadingly, known as Siberian ginseng: more familiar
Panax ginseng is also grown in Siberia. Eleuthero is not a
true ginseng (although it's a member of the same Aralia
family). It has been used in China for more than 2,000
years as an "adaptogen"—a general tonic believed to
enhance longevity. More than 1,000 studies, mostly in
the former Soviet Union, have investigated health
claims for Eleuthero. Enhanced athletic performance
and increased numbers of immune cells were among the
positive findings.

177

Ginseng (*Panax ginseng, P. quinquefolius*) JIN-seng: Strong, rooty, unpleasant taste; strong odor. In tea, usually blended with other herbs or flavoring agents for palatability. Native to China and North America; known as Chinese or Korean ginseng and used medicinally in Asia for more than 5,000 years. A classic Chinese herbal *Pen Tsao Ching* says ginseng enlightens the mind, increases wisdom, and enhances longevity. Latin name, *Panax*, means "panacea" or "cure-all." The fourth-best-selling herb in the United States, ginseng has been the subject of hundreds of clinical and laboratory studies. Methodologies vary, but in the best studies ginseng has been found to improve resistance to stress, reduce fatigue, and enhance mental and physical performance. Ginseng is prescribed in traditional Chinese medicine to improve chronic conditions, strengthen the body to cope with stress, restore vitality, and boost the immune system.

Labrador Tea (*Ledum latifolium, L. groenlandicum*): Native to Greenland and eastern Canada, this evergreen shrub—not related to *Camellia sinensis*, or true tea—was used during the American Revolution as a substitute for black or green tea. It has a pleasant aroma, a spicy taste, and a folk reputation for soothing coughs and indigestion.

Sarsaparilla (*Smilax ornata, S. officinalis*) sass-pa-RILL-ah: The root of a woody vine, sarsaparilla gets its name from two Spanish words: "zarza" (bramble) and "parilla" (vine). It is harvested from wild plants in the tropical forests of Mexico, Jamaica, and Central

America; Spanish traders brought the roots to Europe in the sixteenth century. Once famed as a cure for syphilis and skin disorders, it was the basis of many nineteenth-century tonic cures in the U.S. It has a mild, "root beer" flavor, and is often added to tea blends to improve or balance taste.

Schizandra (*Schizandra sinensis*) shi-ZAN-dra: Fruity and sour; used in tea blends as a counterpoint to sweet herbs. The dried red berries are used. In China, schizandra is known as *wu wei zi*, or "five flavors"—various parts of the fruit have sweet, sour, pungent, bitter, and salty tastes, encompassing all five elements central to Chinese medicine. It is prescribed as an adaptogen and energy tonic, especially useful for conditions of the kidneys and skin.

WHAT'S IN A NAME?

Care for some Quaker's bonnet? How about hoodwort? Or perhaps you'd prefer skullcap or mad-dog weed? In fact, they're all names for the same plant—in botanical nomenclature, Scutellaria lateriflora (literally, "shield-shaped side-flowering"). Swedish botanist Carolus Linneaus, the founder of scientific classification devised the Latin naming system in the eighteenth century, and it continues to help scientists and ordinary folk around the world identify plants and animals.

The first word is the plant's genus, the second word the species. When a plant has several different species, the genus name may be abbreviated to a single letter—for example, Echinacea angustifolia *and* E. purpurea.

"Meanwhile, let us have a sip of tea. The afternoon glow is brightening the bamboos. The fountains are bubbling with delight. The soughing of the pines is heard in our kettle. Let us dream of evanescence. And linger in the beautiful foolishness of things."

—Kakuzo Okakura

Resources for
Further Enjoyment

CHOW, KIT. *All the Tea in China* (San Francisco: China Books and Periodicals Inc., 1990). China-born and Hong Kong-educated Kit Chow began researching tea to improve his health. He uncovered a wealth of fascinating information about the arts and customs of tea as well scientific lore and health benefits.

GRAHAM, PATRICIA J. *The Art of Sencha* (Honolulu: University of Hawai'i Press, 1998). The first English-language study of the Japanese *sencha* (steeped tea) ceremony, an alternative to the more familiar chanoyu. Illustrated.

MCCALEB, ROBERT, et al. *Encyclopedia of Popular Herbs* (Roseville, California: Prima Publishing, 2000). Detailed information, including clinical and laboratory research, in an easy-to-read format; from the Herb Research Foundation.

ODY, PENELOPE. *The Complete Medicinal Herbal* (New York: Dorling Kindersley, Inc., 1993). Practical guide to the healing properties of herbs, written by a respected British herbalist and lavishly illustrated with color photographs.

OKAKURA, KAKUZO. *The Book of Tea* (Boston: Charles E. Tuttle Co., 2000). Beautifully illustrated edition of a modern classic about Japanese tea ceremony, written by a Japanese scholar who relocated to late-nineteenth-century New England and became the curator of East Asian art at the Boston Museum of Fine Arts.

PRATT, JAMES NORWOOD. *New Tea Lover's Treasury* (San Francisco: Publishing Technology Associates, 1999). The result of nearly 20 years of research, written in an engagingly original style and combining history, tasting notes, and lore.

RASMUSSEN, WENDY, and RIC RHINEHART. *Tea Basics: A Quick and Easy Guide* (New York: John Wiley & Sons, 1999). The essentials of tea buying, brewing, and tasting, with a list of resources for tea products. Rasmussen is the executive director of the American Premium Tea Institute.

ROSEN, DIANA. *Chai: The Spice Tea of India* (Pownal, Vermont, Storey Books, 1999). The history and culture of Indian chai, accompanied by charming anecdotes and recipes.

ROSEN, DIANA. *Steeped in Tea: Creative Ideas, Activities & Recipes for Tea Lovers* (Pownal, Vermont, Storey Books, 1999). Suggestions for "tea parties" and projects that include international menus, crafts activities such as tea-dyed curtains, and ideas for incorporating tea into business and personal life.

SCHAPIRA, JOEL, et al. *The Book of Coffee & Tea* (New York: St. Martin's Griffin, second revised edition 1982). A passionately argued guide to caffeinated beverages, written by members of a family with century-old roots in the coffee-roasting and tea-importing business. Still an excellent resource.

SLAVIN, SARA, and KARL PETZKE. *Tea: Essence of the Leaf* (San Francisco: Chronicle Books, 1998). Slim, beautifully designed book with sumptuous color photographs of tea and teawares. Recipes include the exotic (smoky tea prawns) and the cozy (tea scones).

TAYLOR, NADINE. *Green Tea: The Natural Secret for a Healthier Life* (New York: Kensington Books, 1998). A guide to recent research into the health benefits of green tea. Includes glossary and extensive bibliography.

UKERS, WILLIAM H. *All About Tea* (Whitesman, New York: *Tea and Coffee Trade Journal Co.*, 1935). Print-to-order black-and-white reprints of this two-volume classic are available through book search services on the Internet. In many ways it is still the definitive source of information about tea history, culture, literature, and trade. Filled with fascinating illustrations and photos.

Websites

American Premium Tea Institute
www.teainstitute.org
The official Web site of the industry organization. Sample newsletter articles are posted.

British Tea Council
www.teahealth.co.uk
A clearinghouse of information about tea and health.

The Republic of Tea
www.republicoftea.com
Online catalog of fine teas, herbal blends, and teaware.

Herb Research Foundation
www.herbs.org
Dedicated to promoting scientific information about herbs.

Botanical.com
www.botanical.com
The online version of Mrs. Maud Grieve's 1931 *A Modern Herbal*, a comprehensive guide to more than 800 herbs. Includes links to contemporary herbal research.

A Brief History of
The REPUBLIC of TEA

THE REPUBLIC OF TEA is a progressive, socially conscious California company dedicated to enriching people's lives through the experience of tea and the Sip-by-Sip Life—a life of health, balance, and well-being. Its ongoing mission is to seek out and procure only the most exquisite teas and herbs in the world and make them accessible and enjoyable to men, women, and children everywhere.

Launched in 1992 by the founders of Banana Republic, The Republic of Tea was bought in 1994 by Ron Rubin, an entrepreneur committed to expanding the company's mission. He was soon joined by marketing veteran Stuart Avery Gold, and the company soared to national prominence. Today, The Republic's extensive line of teas, herbs, and lifestyle products are available through fine gourmet and specialty food stores, natural groceries, and select department stores, gift stores, cafés, and restaurants throughout North America, and through its award-winning mail order catalog and website (www.republicoftea.com). Their products and innovative packaging have been the recipients of numerous honors and awards.

The story of the Republic's founding is related in *The Republic of Tea: Letters to a Young Zentrepreneur*

185

(Doubleday/Currency, 1994). Ron Rubin and Stuart Avery Gold relate their approach to business and life in *Success @ Life: A Zentrepreneur's Guide—How to Catch and Live Your Dream* (Newmarket Press, 2001). With humor and clarity, Rubin and Gold share their personal experience and their philosophy of "enlightenment and discovery." Their inspired guide has won praise from fellow authors, including: "This is a book—a business book!—filled with grace and beauty and desire. I can offer no higher accolade. Business as passion. Business as cause. Read. Ponder. Act. Contribute. Passionately. Please."—Tom Peters; "This is my kind of book— short, sweet, and to the point. The writing is snappy and fresh, the advice is dead-on, the tea...well, let's just say I'm sipping my way to Zen heaven while I read!"—Cheryl Richardson; "*Success @ Life* is a motivational journey of enlightenment and rediscovery charged with humor, encouragement and entrepreneurial wisdom."—Jeffrey J. Fox

For information about where to purchase the leaves of The Republic of Tea, or for a copy of a mail-order catalog, please contact:

The Republic of Tea
8 Digital Drive, Suite 100
Novato, CA 94949
(800) 298-4832
www.republicoftea.com

Newmarket books are available from your local bookseller or from Newmarket Press, which can be contacted at:

Newmarket Press
18 East 48th Street
New York, NY 10017
(800) 669-3903
FAX (212) 832 3629
e-mail: mailbox@newmarketpress.com
website: www.newmarketpress.com

Acknowledgments

WHAT IS TOLD MAY BE HEARD, BUT EASILY FORGOTTEN.
WHAT IS SHOWN WILL BE SEEN, BUT NOT EASILY REMEMBERED.
FOR THOSE WHO ASPIRE TO KNOW THE WAY, SIP THE TEA.
—THE MINISTER OF TRAVEL

TO BRING A BOOK like this beyond the faraway frontiers would not be possible without the consummate talent of others. The authors would like to thank Nancy Friedman, our Minister of Research, whose hard work graces every page; Caroline MacDougall, Minister of Herbs, for her massive expertise; Barbara Graves, super smart Minister of Commerce, for her passion and dedication; Gina Amador, Minister of Design, for her creative art and imaginative ideas; Heather Innocenti; Michael Spillane; Brian Writer; Allan Shiffrin; Kendra Bochner; Keith Hollaman; Harry Burton; Andrea Brown; Heidi Sachner; Mary Jane DiMassi; Paul Sugarman; Shannon Berning; William Rusin; Dosier Hammond; and Esther Margolis, for her always spiritual advice about the art of publishing.

Index

192